MAKING AMERICA GREAT
THE IMMIGRANT EXPERIENCE

SÉKOU CLARKE

ACKNOWLEDGEMENTS

To begin, I would like to thank God for his continued blessings in my life. None of this would be possible without him.

I would like to thank all the Immigrants whose lives have been stories of inspiration, resilience and persistence. The Immigrant experience could not be told without the sacrifices and shattered glass ceilings of Immigrants in America. I am extremely grateful for Debbie Muse, for her support and professionalism in editing this book and communicating my thoughts to words. Thank you, Andrea and the Scorpion team, for supporting this vision. Huge thanks to Selim Nurudeen for designing a cover that communicates my American Dream. Thank You Kristin for your unyielding support, encouragement and inspiration in me finishing this project. I am extremely grateful for my parents, your prayers, sacrifices and lessons made me the man that I am today. To my staff and friends, I am thankful and humbled by your energy, positivity and encouragement during this journey. Blessup!

Sékou Clarke is the Founder and Managing Attorney of The Sékou Clarke Law Group based in Orlando, Florida. He is passionate about Immigration Law and Injury rights. Sékou immigrated to the United States as a scholarship Track and Field athlete to the University of Florida. During his Track and Field career, Sékou was a Two-Time National champion, multiple time All-American and a member of the Jamaican National Team in track and field. Sékou's Legal journey began in High-School at Jamaica College where he studied English Law and West-Indian and European History in his final year. Sékou is prideful in the meaning of his name-- "warrior", because it embodies who he is and his approach to life.

*"Emancipate yourselves from mental slavery, none but
ourselves can free our minds!"*

— *Marcus* Garvey

CONTENTS

INTRODUCTION

It was July 2014, and I was returning from my first international trip with a United States passport. As the plane slowed to a stop and the seatbelt light blinked off, I felt an immediate sense of relief and even a bit of excitement. For the first time, I would no longer be hassled when returning to the country that I had lived in for over 15 years.

I finally belonged. As I made my way down the aisle, I was already anticipating how it would feel to hear the custom's officer say the words I had always yearned to hear, "welcome home."

Just 30 days prior, traveling back to the U.S. on my Jamaican passport as a legal permanent resident, I was barraged with questions and interrogated for almost an hour.

"Have you been arrested recently?"

"What did you do in Jamaica?"

"Are you bringing back any drugs?"

"Why were you out of the country so long?"

"Do you know it's illegal to lie to an immigration officer?"

"Do you have gang affiliations?"

"How much money do you make?"

This country isn't where I was born, but this is the country I call home. It is the country where I earned my education, secured my first job, launched my own law firm, built my first home and started my family. It is the country that has enabled me to grow, learn and realize my American Dream.

I am an immigrant. I am a proud U.S. citizen. I employ and have been employed by immigrants, and I have been taught by immigrants. Many of us -- U.S citizens and immigrants alike -- can identify with one of these categories. Unfortunately, because of the recent polarization of immigration, the word "immigrant" has been reduced to a classification of the weak, the parasitic, the criminal and the border crossers. In reality, we are your fellow hard workers, taxpayers and veterans; the athletes you fill stadiums to watch; your educators and your neighbors.

I recently had the privilege of mentoring an exceptionally bright 17-year-old intern at my law firm. She was a first-generation Mexican-American, with stellar grades and a relentless work ethic. I asked about her goals for the summer. She responded that she was taking extra classes to graduate early, volunteering and also working a part-time job. I inquired why she was taking on so much when she had already earned multiple college scholarship offers. She told me that she had to overachieve because she saw what her parents sacrificed to get her to this country and how her parents were treated on a daily basis. Overachieving was her solution to breaking the cycle and the stereotype. She shared the ridicule she experienced because she was Mexican, the names she was called, and how hurtful it all was because she was born here in the U.S. just like them. A teenager who was actually born in this country should never feel different or less than because of their familial national origin.

I have three primary goals for this book: 1) to educate U.S. citizens about why an immigrant has rights in this country, 2) to highlight the effects that business owners face with the demolition of immigration laws and 3) to share how immigrants can survive and thrive throughout and beyond President Trump's administration.

The ripples of the "Trump immigration effect" have transcended political lines and affiliations, and the end result is a festering humanitarian crisis. I will always advocate for a red, white and blue nation of laws, and I believe most of us work to maintain this harmony of colors. There is no excuse or place for blatant violation of the rule of law that protects daily life and our future generations. However, whether deliberately or unconsciously, the Trump effect perpetuates the vicious cycle of the empowered preying on the vulnerable and profiting from the disenfranchised and marginalized. It appears the end game is to reduce the red, white and blue to a single hue.

CHAPTER ONE

THE BEGINNING OF AN ERA

The 2016 Campaign

In 2016, then Presidential hopeful Donald Trump decided he would make a bid for the White House. At the time, I was ambivalent to his political posture. Though uncertain, I had some optimism based on his "billionaire mindset" and the business perspective he would bring to developing national economic strategies. Moreover, I knew that at least 11 Trump properties had embraced hundreds of undocumented and documented immigrants for over a decade. So, like most immigrants, I was blindsided when he proposed sweeping immigration changes and his demonization of immigrants infiltrated the media.

Don't get me wrong -- the immigration system needed attention and repair. I am a huge advocate for legal immigration and repercussions for committing crimes, regardless of your immigration status. However, **revamping immigration must be done responsibly and in a bi-partisan manner, and not at the expense of isolating, marginalizing and labelling a group of people based on their national origin.**

The Trump campaign seemingly galvanized a loyal base in 2016, with promises of walls, travel bans, and the removal of "11 million" undocumented immigrants currently living in the United States. The most aggressive and controversial actions proved evident in the rise of detention centers, the Family Separation Policy, Immigration and Customs Enforcement (ICE) raids, and the phasing out of Deferred Action for Childhood Arrivals (DACA) just name a few. However, the most undeniable shift is the way Americans began to view immigration and immigrants.

The 2020 Campaign

Reflecting on 2020, I can't help but think back to the nights of laying in my room as a teenager, dreaming and planning how to get to the United States. I didn't imagine the United States as an escape from my beloved home country of Jamaica; I dreamed of going to the United States because, at the time, I knew I could achieve my best self. I believed that my work ethic was unmatched and that the right opportunity would allow me to build my American Dream.

This dream was not living in the house with the white picket fence. It was owning the bustling downtown office building with the gleaming glass walls and working in the corner office. My American Dream was having the liberty and resources to not only have a home and safety for my family, but to create generational security and stability. My American Dream has and will always be the freedom to pursue and achieve my definition of peace and happiness -- not because of where I am from or what I look like, but because I sacrificed, worked hard and earned it.

In his run for re-election, Trump continued to make immigration a focal point of his presidential platform, focusing on illegal immigration, border security and reforming the existing legal immigration system. And why not? The loyal Trump base loves this! The narrative that immigrants take jobs from vulnerable Americans, drain social services and harm innocent families continued despite the glaring statistic from the chief actuary of the Social Security Administration that undocumented workers have paid an estimated $100 billion in Social Security taxes over the last decade.

Throughout the Trump years, my greatest concern has become the targeting of not just undocumented immigrants and asylum seekers, but legal immigrants and naturalized citizens as well. Yes, I said naturalized citizens! The goal post is moving. In February 2020, the Trump administration created a new denaturalization "task force" under the Department of Justice. I can completely understand and support the rationale behind bringing to justice terrorists, war criminals, sex offenders and other fraudsters who illegally obtained naturalization. However, the repercussions to the masses may outweigh the benefits. Countless people will lose their citizenship due to legal procedural errors. However, the biggest effect is that naturalized U.S. citizens now live in fear, are vulnerable to an assault of their citizenship, and are relegated to the feeling of being treated as second-class citizens, regardless of the dues they have paid to this country.

I can jump on the bandwagon of revamping the current immigration system and addressing illegal immigration in a humane and fair way. However, I doubt the additional impacts of retroactively pursuing immigrants have been reasonably calculated. Like myself, most immigrants didn't come to the United States for hand-outs or to live a mediocre life -- most came because they believed that they could add value to the "American Dream." After all, didn't our founders promise a "Land of Opportunity?"

CHAPTER TWO

IMMIGRATION CHANGES UNDER PRESIDENT TRUMP

One of the defining moments of my life was signing my letter of intent to attend the University of Florida on an athletic scholarship. It was a dream come true for many reasons. This accomplishment meant that I was one step closer to going to the United States to not only pursue my love of running, but more importantly, my dream of seizing the opportunities that the United States promised. Have you ever wondered why students, athletes and professionals leave their home countries to come to the United States? When you live outside the U.S., you can't get away from it. You grow up seeing the American way of life on TV and in magazines that line the grocery store checkout shelves. As an outsider, you can't help but believe and think that America is the "gold standard," the pinnacle of achieving success.

As a result of polarizing rhetoric and images, most Americans agree with and demand changes to the current immigration system. They believe that immigrants are invading our nation's borders, taking jobs and increasing crime. In 2020, the problem hit a new height when many Americans started believing that the label "immigrant" is synonymous with border crossers and second-class citizens who feed on an already strained welfare system. The label "immigrant" now means "not-American," regardless of what your passport says. The hypocrisy is that the label immigrant is ignored and camouflaged in everyday American life when it seemingly benefits Americans. A recent study by New American Economy found that:

- In 2019, immigrant-owned businesses employed almost 8 million American workers and generated $1.3 trillion in total sales.

- Immigrants comprise one in every five entrepreneurs in the country, with 3.2 million immigrants running their own businesses.

- Between 2016 and 2017, the number of immigrant homeowners grew by 4.6 percent, from 9.1 million to 9.5 million.

- Households led by immigrants earned $1.5 trillion in total income and contributed $405 billion in tax revenues to federal, state, and local governments, leaving them with $1.1 trillion in spending power.

Despite these statistics, many Americans stereotype immigrants and perceive them as a burden. Yet, throughout our country's history, immigrants have served as the foundation of the American Dream. Nonetheless, Trump has not disappointed with bulldozing long-standing immigration safeguards and implementing damaging new immigration laws.

Family-based Immigration

During President Trump's State of the Union address in 2018, he outlined a four-pillar plan that would make significant cuts to the country's family-based immigration system. Under the proposed plan, immigrants who become citizens or legal permanent residents would no longer be allowed to sponsor parents, siblings, children and spouses for green cards. Instead, immigrants granted citizenship can only sponsor spouses and minor children. According to data from the Migration Policy Institute, Trump's plan would eliminate 317,661 family-based green cards.

In June 2020, Trump expanded and extended his immigration ban, which directly affects family-based immigrant visas. Among the categories affected, the parents of U.S. citizens who are outside of the country are now restricted for a period of time. This ban was implemented under the rhetoric that it is a necessary evil to protect American jobs that had been compromised due to the Covid-19 pandemic.

Family reunification has long been a hallmark of the American Dream, and depending on your perspective, the vision or interpretation of the Founding Fathers. Most immigrants like myself work that much harder and make more professional sacrifices because of their family values and desire to have their families by their sides, just like most American-born citizens. Trump has repeatedly called this chain migration, but I see this as strengthening the American chain. People will always be stronger, more resourceful and live more fulfilling lives when they are surrounded by their family.

Employment-based Immigration

If H.R. 1044, the Fairness for High-Skilled Immigrants Act of 2019, passes, it will reduce the wait times for visas by getting rid of per-country caps for employment-based green cards. However, the Senate has also proposed an amendment that will create tighter restrictions on recruitment and new reporting requirements for H-1B visa sponsors.

Investor Visas

In addition, President Trump's administration made substantial changes to the EB-5 Immigrant Investor Visa program that went into effect on November 11, 2019. The changes include the following:

- The minimum investment amount has been raised to $1.8 million.

- The minimum investment amount for targeted employment areas (TEAs) has been raised to $900,000.

- States can no longer designate certain geographic and political subdivisions as high-unemployment areas.

- EB-5 petitioners can keep their priority date if they have a previously approved petition.

CHAPTER THREE

WORLD POWER AND WORLD RESPONSIBILITY

Asylum and DACA

I can't speak for other attorneys, but for me, my client stories are what drive me the most. As a relatively young attorney, I still grapple with not physically or mentally taking cases home with me, and I will never forget a particular client consultation I did. The client was a woman in her early to mid-twenties, humbly but confidently dressed, and well spoken. As the consult unfolded, I began to question the woman, listening keenly as her accent was heavy, but her words were eloquent. She began her story by sharing her fear of returning to her home country. As I continued to question her about this fear, her initial posture of confidence deflated. The woman began to shiver as she told me stories of being chased in her home country, hiding from her attackers, and self-treating her wounds. She then proceeded to show me the scars on her neck and waist from the stab wounds she had endured. I couldn't grasp how as a human race, we could be so cruel. This woman was targeted and persistently attacked in her home country because of her religion and sexuality.

Her government offered no form of protection and seemingly encouraged such treatment.

Fast forward to approximately 18 months after that initial consultation and one asylum application later, and the woman returned to my office just to say hello. She exuded confidence as she told me about her new job promotion and proudly showed me her keys to her own apartment and new car. She was also excited to be starting school to pursue her business degree. Witnessing this metamorphosis and example of human perseverance, I wept tears of joy and pride.

In today's America, the term "asylum" has been diluted and stigmatized. The Trump administration's narrative became that asylum status is one of the most abused mediums of immigration. With any immigration process and system that offers a benefit in the U.S., there is abuse. That said, I advocate an asylum process and procedure that efficiently vets the abuse and persecution asylum applicants have experienced.

Most Americans tend to question the need for asylum or ask why it's America's problem to provide a safe haven for persecuted people from other countries when Americans have to take care of so many of their "own people." As I said earlier, I love the patriotism of Americans. However, this patriotism should not be selective. The U.S. is a world power because of its global principles of freedom and equality. We are the "land of the free and the home of the brave," right? The U.S. earned this title by fighting for freedom and providing a safe-haven for the persecuted.

Following World War II, most nations throughout the world agreed to offer asylum to victims of persecution to prevent a recurrence of anything similar to what the Jews experienced fleeing Nazi Germany during the Holocaust. The U.S. stepped up and provided a safe haven for Jewish refugees. In 1951, the United Nations adopted the Convention Relating to the Status of Refugees. According to this agreement (signed by the United States and codified in U.S. law in 1980), qualified refugees who can reach a "safe country" have the right to be given shelter and granted asylum in that country.

What Asylum Was Like in the U.S. Before the Trump Era

In the past, asylum has been available to immigrants who fled their country of origin and were afraid to return because they feared for their lives. Asylum seekers were granted formal protections in the U.S. with the signing of the Refugee Act of 1980, which established a federal system for admitting asylum seekers into the country. Under the act, immigrants granted asylum status are allowed to apply for permanent residence after living in the U.S. for one year. They can also obtain a social security card and legally work for U.S. employers. It is important to note that immigrants are allowed to apply regardless of whether they legally or illegally entered the country.

However, new restrictions enacted during Trump's presidency make it more difficult to make asylum claims.

Asylum Changes Under the Trump Administration

Trump has referred to asylum seekers at the Southern border as the "scam" and has long argued that immigrants take advantage of the asylum system by making false claims to secure legal protections. Seemingly, this narrative was applied with a broad brush to zero in on people from South and Central America. However, the evident result of targeting people by national origin is the exclusion and subliminal discrimination these groups of people now face.

I will always remember one of my South-American clients who was a green card holder for 10 years and a senior physician at her local hospital in Michigan. She shared with me that since Trump arrived on the political scene, she preferred to live in her scrubs, because when she wore regular clothes and had any type of daily conflict at the gas station, Department of Motor Vehicles or grocery store check-out line, people would be quick to say, "Go back to where you come from" or "We speak English here." They uttered these insults not knowing that this woman is saving American lives and often putting her own life at risk to do so. Despite being an asylee and enduring the increased negative rhetoric hurled at her, she still speaks with pride about helping people regardless of where they are from or how they look. She said she does it because she took an oath as a doctor, and to her, saving lives is the right thing and the American thing to do.

During his time as president, Trump's administration decided to change the way asylum applications are processed, prioritizing recently-filed asylum applications over applications that have been pending for years. The policy has been referred to as "last in, first out." The Trump administration also announced that asylum seekers would be required to first seek asylum from one of the countries they pass through on their journey to the U.S. Under this new rule, asylum seekers are only offered legal protection in the U.S. if the claims made in other countries they passed through are denied. This means migrants traveling to the U.S from Central America have to apply for asylum with at least one country they pass through on their journey. If the asylum claim made in another country is denied, they can petition for asylum at a U.S. port of entry.

Then, in June 2020, the Trump administration proposed regulations with "adverse factors" that may count against asylum applicants. The regulations state that living unlawfully in the U.S. for more than a year prior to filing for asylum would be considered a "significant adverse factor." In addition, the failure to file taxes or having a criminal conviction, regardless if it was reversed, vacated or expunged, may count against an individual's asylum claim.

These sweeping asylum changes not only go against the traditions and long-standing history of American culture, but also create a vacuum for immigrants already here. History has not favored a marginalized group of people already in the country. As an immigrant, I am wholeheartedly behind refining immigration laws to benefit the immigrant who is escaping persecution and the immigrant who will contribute to the American Dream. However, there is a growing fear for and amongst immigrants because the term "immigrant" is becoming a cue to label, target and minimalize a subcategory of people.

DACA

I recently met with a family that had two sons born one and a half years apart. Both boys are ambitious and were busy sending out college and internship applications. They expressed that it had been a bittersweet mixture of feelings because the older son was a Deferred Action for Childhood Arrivals (DACA) applicant and the other was a U.S. citizen. However, the parents decided to raise them both without telling them about their relative status. I asked the parents why they took this approach, and they responded that they wanted both children to grow up feeling equal and limitless. Now that the boys are 17 and 18, and want to travel and explore college and internship opportunities locally and internationally, the parents are terrified that the limitations and uncertainty of DACA will crush their eldest son's dream of truly experiencing adulthood. He knows no other country but the U.S., has never been to his parent's home country of Peru and is as American as Instagram selfies.

Since I became a parent, I have a new awareness and appreciation of the desire to defend and protect your child by all means necessary. As parents, we absorb the responsibility of making decisions on behalf of our children without their approval or consent about 90 percent of the time. Why? Because we are the adults with the advantage of life experience. The value of family is a high commodity in most immigrant families. So, it is of no surprise that immigrants will go through great lengths to bring children to the U.S., even if it is illegal. When it comes to providing a better life for your child, the reward is always seemingly greater than the risk.

In 2012, the Differed Action for Childhood Arrivals (DACA) was born. DACA permitted certain juveniles who came to the United States and met set criteria to obtain temporary legal status. Lacking current lawful immigration status, they could request consideration of deferred action for a period of two years, subject to renewal and eligibility for work authorization.

The Trump administration made attempts to dismantle the DACA program, claiming that it was illegal and unconstitutional with no other justification. With the current tide of immigration, some Americans will support the end of DACA on the basis that it will reduce illegal immigration, that "they" should not have been here to begin with, and that "they" are putting a burden on social programs.

The overlooked statistic is that thousands of these children, who are often called "Dreamers," have come to rely on DACA. Many emerged from the safety net of DACA to enroll in degree programs, embark on careers, start businesses, buy homes, marry and have 200,000 children of their own who are U.S. citizens. But most importantly, since 2012, DACA recipients have paid $60 billion in taxes each year.

My contention to cancelling DACA is simple -- these immigrants have been in the United States since they were children by no choice of their own. They only know America. Many have made great contributions to our country and are now woven into the American fabric.

As a superpower, the United States has set the trend for freedom of choice and rewarding hard work with tangible success. In fact, the U.S. achieved much of its success through a blind acceptance of hard work -- hard work that was accepted regardless of where you came from or how you got here as long as the work was done well and added value. Hard work is the fuel of dreams -- the dreams of the Dreamers.

CHAPTER FOUR

IMMIGRATION AND THE U.S. CONSTITUTION

According to Article I, Section 8 of the U.S. Constitution, Congress has the responsibility "to establish a uniform Rule of Naturalization" that determines the process immigrants must go through to become citizens of the United States. It is arguably the biggest, unequivocal shout-out that immigration receives from the U.S. Constitution. Making Congress responsible for immigration directly made immigration a federal issue, thus taking the issue of naturalization away from the states.

Over the years, the majority of immigration changes have been created through legislation. This includes the Nationality Act of 1790, the 1882 Chinese Exclusion Act, the Immigration Act of 1891, the Immigration Act of 1924, the 1966 Cuban Refugee Adjustment, the Refugee Act of 1980, and the Deferred Action of Childhood Arrivals (DACA) in 2012 (executive action), just to name a few. Without boring you with the details of all the acts, they have a common theme. Each act from the 1700's until now set out to accommodate and provide opportunities for immigrants, establishing that immigrants have always been a part of the conversation in the United States. However, each accommodating act tends to be followed by an act that puts a limit, exclusion or burden that immigrants must meet.

This saga continues today. Immigration laws are created to accommodate immigrants, but then subsequent laws are enacted to limit and remove the immigrants that the previous law created, which then creates an increase in illegal immigration. DACA and asylum feel very familiar.

The only notable thing that has changed in 2020 is that instead of creating guidelines to accommodate deserving immigrants already in the U.S., immigrants have been labeled, politicized and deemed "the problem of America." In my opinion, it's laughable to think that a wall will solve the problem, and it is heart-wrenching to think sub-human detention centers are an alternative solution. However, it's far worse to perpetuate a narrative that immigrants are a sub-category of people with more cons than pros to the U.S. economy. With over 30 acts of legislation addressing immigration over three centuries, the law continues to view immigrants as temporary, disposable people instead of assets.

As a child growing up in Jamaica, I was always a student and fanatic of history. In my latter years of high school, I became captivated by West Indian and European History in particular. My fascination of past journeys to civilization and freedom has always served as a foundation, inspiration and roadmap to how I envisioned life and society.

When I became a law student and was introduced to U.S. Constitutional law, it was no different. I couldn't get enough of the process of putting U.S. history into the context of court cases that created the "laws of the land." My greatest conundrum after a two-semester battle with constitutional law was the debate of the intent of the "framers" when creating the U.S. Constitution versus the Constitution's interpretation and application today. Many constitutional scholars and judges defer to theories of contextualism, originalism and constructionism (to name a few) to interpret the intent of certain laws within the Constitution.

Despite being thoroughly impressed that a group of men had the foresight to intricately construct such a governing document in the 1700's, I am baffled that a nation could still be governed by a document that was written over three centuries ago. Most would agree that the United States the Framers envisioned then is a completely different United States in 2020. Do you think James Madison could have envisioned making a TikTok video? Nonetheless, I still believe in the structure, governance and culture afforded by the U.S. Constitution, and it is arguably one of the greatest documents ever constructed. Conversely, I also believe that the representation, values and beliefs of the 39 men in 1789 who signed the Constitution are starkly different from today's demographic melting pot of free men, bold women and eclectic religious views. I also don't believe John Adams could envision that the journey to the Constitutional Convention could be accomplished in a Zoom meeting today. However, I do believe James Madison, aka the father of the Constitution, had the foresight to speak about immigrants when he said, **"the purpose of the Constitution is to restrict the majority's ability to harm a minority."**

CHAPTER FIVE

CONSTITUTIONAL RIGHTS OF UNDOCUMENTED IMMIGRANTS

As an immigrant, I have always been fascinated with the tangible sense of patriotism in the U.S. This sense of "belonging" to a country and culture that has well-defined laws that are historically empowered by a document written centuries ago can be seen, heard and felt. The liberties afforded to U.S. citizens should be relished and never taken for granted. In fact, these freedoms are the primary reason immigrants seek the borders of this country, and arguably, are the reason that the U.S. is still viewed as a "world leader." However, the liberties and protections afforded by the Constitution beg the question, **is the constitutional language being interpreted as the Framers intended or is the enforcement of the Constitution selective?**

The Bill of Rights, particularly the Fourteenth Amendment, provides protection and safeguards for all Americans. The Framers actually thought that for any growing Democratic nation, there needed to be protection from its own government – the operative word being "protection." Some of these protections are from government restrictions on freedom of speech, detention without due process, and discrimination on the basis of religion and ethnicity to name a few.

I believe that the Framers could not envision a black president with a name like Barack Obama as the elected Commander in Chief. Therefore, I can only go out on a limb and assume that when the Framers were sent to the Constitutional Convention in Philadelphia in the summer of 1787, they did not foresee the immigrant fabric of our nation today. Therefore, the Framers' intent was for the Constitution to protect and govern all people on U.S. soil.

I'm now running with this assumption to challenge the "intent" or the application of the word "people" as opposed to the omission of the word "citizens" in the framing of the U.S. Constitution. More importantly, **I'm challenging how the use of the word "people" is being interpreted and applied today.**

Stay with me. The U.S. Constitution starts off with the patriotic words, *"We the People,"* and the First Amendment ensures "the right of the people" to petition the government and to peacefully assemble. The Second Amendment protects "the right of the people" to keep and bear arms, and the Fourth Amendment protects "the right of the people" against unreasonable searches and seizures. The Ninth and Tenth Amendments reserve to "the people" non-enumerated rights and powers. This leads to my perhaps obvious pivot -- an assumption that many rights afforded by the U.S. Constitution to Americans were meant to apply to immigrants, whether documented or undocumented. Or are those rights selectively interpreted in 2020?

One of the most common phrases used in social uprisings, protests or even just trying to get out of a traffic ticket is, "I know my rights." These are very American words and are often valid. Many people feel like they are taken more seriously when saying them. However, the rights afforded by the Constitution to Americans are also afforded to "people," and yes, "people" includes immigrants. **However, these rights tend to get complicated when putting the laws into practice.**

You might say, "obviously people refers to legal people in this country." This may be a valid point. However, the cherished rights we enjoy from the

U.S. Constitution offer protections to all people on U.S. soil, regardless of immigration status.

The Right to Due Process

Jilmar Ramos-Gomez served in the U.S. Marines and completed tours in Afghanistan. He was born in Grand Rapids, Michigan, and was a U.S. citizen in every sense of the word. However, after suffering PTSD, he had a minor run-in with law enforcement, resulting in a trespassing charge. After his release from Kent County jail, Jilmar was turned over to Immigration and Customs Enforcement (ICE) on the false basis that he was in the country illegally and was subject to removal proceedings. Luckily, the Marine war veteran did not suffer the full fate of ICE's egregious error. An attorney intervened and vindicated Jilimar. However, thousands of Americans will suffer as a result of mass deportation and the wrath of human error.

The Fifth Amendment states that "no person ... shall be compelled in any criminal case to be a witness against himself, nor be deprived of life, liberty, or property, without due process of law." Due process is a constitutional guarantee that all legal proceedings against someone will be fair, proper notice of the proceedings will be provided, and the person will have an opportunity to be heard before their rights are taken away.

The constitutional right of immigrants as it pertains to due process has become a growing concern. Generally, the immigration court is the only arena where an immigrant can be legally removed under proper due process. An immigrant is given a notice to appear and an opportunity to be heard before their right to be in the country is taken away by deportation.

Unfortunately, in 2017, we saw the expansion of **expedited removal**. This allowed immigrants to be removed from the country without an opportunity to be heard. Since 2019, expedited removal may be applied to undocumented immigrants, those who have committed fraud or misrepresentation, and those who are encountered within the United States and who have not been physically present in the country for two years prior to apprehension.

The issue with the expansion of expedited removal is that removal of an immigrant's right is no longer heard by an immigration judge, but is instead heard by an immigration officer. This low-level officer is given the role of prosecutor and judge, regardless if the immigrant has an attorney or not. The only exception is asylum seekers, who must be granted a hearing.

In my mind, this is tantamount to a worker at the DMV, who may be having a bad day, deciding not to let you pay your ticket when you clearly have all of the required paperwork. However, in this instance, instead of getting points on your driver's license, your fate is being deported. Despite Justice Antonin Scalia stating, "it is well established that the Fifth Amendment entitles aliens to due process of law in deportation proceedings," expedited removal has become a reality.

The loss of liberty is another broken constitutional promise for immigrants. The 1993 Supreme Court case, *Reno v. Flores*, created the guidelines for detaining and releasing immigrant children. Generally, they required the government to release children to their parents, a relative or a licensed program within 20 days. However, the challenge for the federal government was deciding if children should be detained with parents or if children should be released and the parents detained. I completely understand that there will be immigrants who take advantage of a system and that there are immigrants who, based on their history, don't deserve to enter the country. However, what I can't support is the need for legislation to determine whether detained children get food, drinking water and soap. There is no easy solution, but there is a clear one. It should be a priority to release arriving children from detention as soon as safely possible. If we can't provide basic life and liberty to children, do you really think there is hope for adult immigrants?

The Right to an Attorney

As a young attorney, I remember sitting in an immigration court waiting for my client's case to be heard. On that particular day, I was sitting through another proceeding. All I could hear was the heavy Eastern European accent of a middle-aged man trying to defend himself against removal. Everything the man said in his defense was wrong, but I could not ignore the deafening sound of his fight. I could hear the man's very soul in his voice when he explained how he had been in the country for 20 years with no arrests until now and had successfully raised a family. However, he was faced with losing everything because he was not adequately represented. I did the natural thing that any attorney with youthful exuberance would do -- I stood up and asked the man if I could represent him. He was baffled. I'm not sure if it was because I was a young black man in a suit coming to his aid or because it was a lifeline he desperately needed. In the end, I was happy to represent him. He asked me why I felt the need to help, and I told him we are all immigrants at the end of the day, and in America, everyone deserves to have an attorney in court.

The Sixth Amendment states that a person facing criminal accusations shall be represented by an attorney. This means that undocumented immigrants also have the right to obtain legal counsel in all criminal proceedings. The Supreme Court ruled in the 1963 case *Gideon v. Wainwright* that if a person cannot afford to hire an attorney, the government must appoint one. Therefore, if a U.S. citizen is faced with criminal prosecution, or more specifically, felony charges, and is found to be "indigent" or "poor," they will be appointed a public defender. Yes, the same constitutional liberty is afforded to undocumented immigrants.

However, the challenge that an undocumented immigrant will face is that most deportation proceedings are civil rather than criminal cases. Therefore, the right to legal counsel often doesn't apply. The next challenge immigrants face is that criminal state charges tend to automatically trigger ICE holds and the need go through immigration court proceedings separately from state criminal court. In this case, as one can imagine, the government will not provide an attorney for the undocumented immigrant. Speaking with my attorney hat on, if you do commit a crime knowing your immigration status is less than legal, you, not U.S. taxpayers, should pay in every sense of the word.

Nonetheless, undocumented immigrants have the absolute right to retain private counsel for criminal and immigration proceedings, and while on U.S. soil, this right should not be infringed upon.

Access to Education for Immigrant Children

One of my absolute favorite clauses in the U.S. Constitution is the Equal Protection Clause from the Fourteenth Amendment. It states, "nor shall any State [...] deny to any person within its jurisdiction the equal protection of the laws." The Equal Protection Clause requires that all individuals have equal footing and equal protection under the law, regardless of what they look like or from where they came. In my opinion, and unknowingly to most immigrants, the Equal Protection Clause is one of the fundamental protections that MAKES AMERICA GREAT.

Regardless of the Framers' original intent, it is written in law that a person, by theory, cannot be discriminated against because of their race, religion, gender, illegitimacy, national origin or alienage.

To most Americans, this theory, and I intentionally use the word "theory" due to its questionable application in reality, is everyday life. To the immigrant, this theory of equality is a sign of hope --hope in the sense that regardless of who you are or the culture you are from, you will have an opportunity. Hope is not a daily reality in other countries -- your opportunities can be legally limited by your gender, your race or by belonging to a certain identifiable group.

For most Americans, it is easy to assume that the majority of immigrants come to the U.S. to escape or to obtain an easier life. But in reality, most immigrants come because of the promise of hope, life and liberty -- a promise that is in the same document that created the greatness of this country. Embedded in this promise is the opportunity of education.

The strength of any nation is directly correlated to access to education for its children. I once met a Venezuelan family, where between the two parents, they had seven degrees. The father was a bio-chemist and the mother an engineer. During our first consultation, where they were seeking a specialized immigrant visa based on their advanced degrees, this couple was less concerned about their soon-to-be expired status and more concerned about the welfare of their three young children who were all under the age of 10. Because of their own educational achievements, these parents recognized the value of an education. The family came to the U.S. because they knew that their knowledge and professional experience provided something to offer. Yet, their greatest concern was their children's ability to secure an education while they sought legal residency.

Children are the beginning and end of every civilization. In the same breath, children are also the most vulnerable population because of their inability to consent, provide for themselves and decide the status they will have in a country. The fair and equal protections also apply to educational access for immigrant children. The Equal Protection Clause logic is that if U.S. citizens can receive free schooling, so should others. Even detention facilities that house children must provide health care, education and other services. The U.S. Supreme Court ruled in *Plyler v. Doe* (457 U.S. 202 (1982)) that undocumented children and young adults have the same right to attend public, primary and secondary schools as do U.S. citizens and permanent residents. Like other children, undocumented students are obliged under state law to attend school until they reach a mandated age. As the law of the land, the Plyer ruling, has determined that public schools may not:

1. Deny admission to a student during initial enrollment or at any other time on the basis of undocumented status

2. Treat a student differently to determine residency

3. Engage in any practices to "chill" the right of access to school

4. Require students or parents to disclose or document their immigration status

5. Make inquiries of students or parents that may expose their undocumented status

6. Require social security numbers from all students as this may expose undocumented status. (Adults without social security numbers who are applying for the free/reduced lunch or breakfast program on behalf of a student need only indicate on the application that they do not have a Social Security number.)

Why should U.S. taxpayers have to pay for the illegal decisions and actions of immigrants bringing their children into the country? Courts, legal minds and myself all agree that preventing children within U.S. borders from an education will only result in the further expansion of an uneducated class. This leads to additional long-term problems such as unemployment and potential welfare costs. Based on recent rhetoric, the solution to this problem is creating walls, bans and completely shutting down borders to prevent this problem from even starting.

In 2020, there cannot and should not be a broad, one-size-fits-all method of determining which people should be prevented or allowed to enter this country. More importantly, race, religion or national origin should NOT be the determining factor when deciding who comes into the country (i.e., immigration policies). A fair immigration policy should be should be founded on the benefit the immigrant brings to this nation, the protection the immigrant needs when faced with persecution and mortal danger, and the ability to provide that protection. This foundation must be implemented with a formulated series of checks and balances, and a vetting process that is applied uniformly for the protection of the U.S.

We as U.S. citizens must understand that the U.S. did not become a world leader exclusively by the way we treated our own citizens. The U.S. became a world leader by the way the U.S. treated the world.

CHAPTER SIX

FAMILY SEPARATION VS. THE RIGHT TO BE WITH FAMILY

I vividly remember one of my very first immigration court cases. I was retained during the final stages of removal proceedings, and I received no details on the case. I just knew that the client was bringing the file to my office five days before the court hearing. To my amazement, when the client came to my office, it was a 13-year-old Central American girl. I'll call her Linda. I asked Linda where her parents were, and she said that her mother was sent back to Guatemala and her father was taken by ICE. She explained that she enjoyed school here and that the conditions living with her aunt were much better than living in Guatemala. Linda shared that she enjoyed her iPhone, Disney movies and going to the parks. Nonetheless, the meeting was difficult -- not because she didn't have a case, but because I could see a deep sadness within her that was covered up by faint smiles. She became very emotional as we began discussing her parents. One thing she said has stuck with me for years: "America means nothing if I can't be with my parents."

The true strength of a nation is its ability to support and protect its people and families. Basic human life is founded on families born from blood, culture or love. Most people are guided by principles learned when they were children. One of the greatest tragedies in recent years has been the politicization of immigration. When you're an immigrant and experience the maze of the U.S. immigration process, your currency and lifeline is hope -- not a ballot or party line. Immigration should be a bi-partisan issue with bi-partisan resolutions because the issue and the affected are people.

One of the most galvanizing effects of the Trump administration's immigration efforts has been the separation of immigrant families. It has been reasoned that that these are "illegal families" breaking the law to come into the country, and therefore, they assumed the risk. As an immigrant, father and attorney, I simply cannot agree with that rhetoric. Children should not be punished for the decisions of their adult parents or worse, taken from their parents and punished for their parent's "wrong doings."

Under previous administrations, families were typically paroled into the country to await their immigration cases, or parents and children were detained together. In 2017, under a pilot program in El Paso, Texas, immigrants illegally crossing the border were criminally charged with a misdemeanor offense (for first-time offenders) and detained. The downward spiral began when parents illegally crossed the border with young children, and the children were separated from the parents. It then snowballed because parents were unable to locate or reunite with their children. At the time, the government had no efficient reunification system or strategy in place.

It doesn't matter your political beliefs or your level of patriotism, one can empathize with the fear and the emotional trauma any child experiences when losing their parents – even if it is just at the local mall for 30 minutes. Now imagine you are a young child, in a new country and an unfamiliar environment, and you witness your parents being taken away. You are now alone and confined with strangers for weeks to months.

The Right of Family

In my daily battles as an attorney, when I have my sword and shield down, I often find myself counseling and giving advice to my clients. There is the client who is faced with voluntary departure or remaining in ICE custody to fight his removal proceeding so that he can stay in the U.S. to see his children graduate from college. There is the wife who has to wait an additional year to see her spouse because of an internal USCIS error. No matter what the case, my counsel always comes from a place of compassion first and legal boundaries second.

In two very historic court decisions, *Meyer v. State of Nebraska* and *Pierce, Governor of Oregon, et al.*, the courts determined that "the Constitution protects the sanctity of the family precisely because the institution of the family is deeply rooted in this nation's history and tradition."

The U.S. Constitution protects the people, the right to marry and the right to parent. Although it is not highlighted in a specific amendment, every person on U.S. soil has the fundamental right to be with their family. It could be successfully argued that a government agency intentionally separating family members, irrespective of immigration status, is unconstitutional unless it was for emergency reasons such as child abuse.

CHAPTER SEVEN

THE TRUMP ADMINISTRATION'S ZERO-TOLERANCE IMMIGRATION POLICY

Uncontrolled and mismanaged immigration policies can lead to irreversible problems in any nation.

One potential challenge that immigration poses is the introduction of a culturally different base of people into the country.

This mass integration produces a situation where people's legal status cannot be accounted for in real time.

Unaccounted people, in a seemingly structured nation, pose a potential burden on government resources because of their ambiguous and unmonitored status. Business owners may see this as an advantage and employ this category of people at a lower cost, reducing the availability of jobs to legal residents and citizens.

Immigration also brings the potential of increased criminal activity.

Sadly, the statements above are the perception of immigration that many Americans hold today. Of course, there are downsides to everything, but what is the upside of integration of a culturally different base of people? Well, the United States was built on culturally different perspectives and has benefited from a competitive workforce that produces a higher standard of work product as a result of the integration of culturally diverse people. Immigration and its effects have created a robust workforce that fuels every sector of the U.S. economy. For example, recent research conducted by New American Economy showed that in 2017, immigrants contributed $920 million to the gross domestic product (GDP) of the Longview, Texas metropolitan area. In addition to their financial contributions, they paid $46.9 million in federal taxes and $29.0 million in state and local taxes. Moving further west, immigrant-owned Tesla directly and indirectly generated $5.5 billion in economic impact and 50,000 jobs to the state of California. And yes, Elon Musk is an immigrant. You don't get to choose which immigrants to keep simply based on their national origin.

The private sector depends on human capital and ingenuity from diverse ideas. No matter how you slice it, the reality is that every nation thrives on immigration. However, it has to be implemented and enforced uniformly and with a bipartisan approach because immigration isn't simply a policy governing manufactured parts or raw materials, it is governing human lives.

On April 6, 2018, the Trump Administration introduced its **"zero-tolerance" policy for criminal illegal entry**. It promised to increase the criminal prosecution of immigrants who illegally enter the United States. The administration stated that this was a necessary policy to secure the border and maintain public safety, national security and the rule of law. However, as previously mentioned, the application of a broad method to restrict people by race, religion and national origin creates additional problems. Obviously, if you're focusing solely on U.S. border crossings, you're narrowly targeting a small cross-section of people. How effective or targeted is this policy if it has been statistically proven and litigated that most illegal immigration occurs from immigrants who enter the country legally and overstay their visas?

And guess what, they aren't from border countries as has been depicted in recent years.

Based on a 2019 report by the Center for Migration Studies, "Visa overstays have significantly outnumbered migrants that enter the country illegally at the Southern border every year since 2007. When juxtaposed to the number of total visa overstays, there were 600,000 more than the total number of border crossers. Therefore, visa overstays accounted for two-thirds of all new undocumented immigrants."

So, what is the end game of this immigration policy? If the numbers don't match the rhetoric, why target the border? I can only deduce that it is easy to label illegal immigration as Mexicans crossing the border. It makes for a simple, familiar narrative. However, it is baseless and wrong.

CHAPTER EIGHT

IMPACTS OF THE ZERO-TOLERANCE POLICY

It is no surprise that taking a grenade approach to a narrow issue has explosive effects.

During my second meeting with Linda, my 13-year-old Guatemalan client, she tearfully described her memory of holding on to her father as the ICE agent pulled her away from him. She shared that before that day, she never knew her dad could cry. She went on to describe how her father begged the ICE agents just to let him hug her one more time as they dragged him into the back of a white van and closed the doors. She expressed that she was so confused because she knew her father wasn't a criminal and never did anything wrong.

In 2018, the United States Department of Health and Human Services reported that approximately 3,000 children were separated from their parents. The zero-tolerance policy has resulted in undocumented immigrant parents, from targeted regions, being apprehended regardless of if they had minors or expressed fear of returning to their home countries. They were sent to federal prison facilities, and their children were separated from them. The ripple effects of this policy spawned the rise of detention centers and a humanitarian crisis involving the poor treatment of undocumented immigrant children.

On June 20, 2018, President Trump signed an Executive Order to stop family separation among undocumented immigrants crossing the border. Nonetheless, the "zero-tolerance" policy is still in effect. The Trump Administration also communicated that these laws were already in place in prior administrations and that the Trump administration was simply implementing existing laws. However, past administrations typically prosecuted people only if they had serious prior criminal convictions and had reentered after being deported or if they were "repeat offenders" who had reentered after deportation. In addition, past administrations also targeted undocumented immigrants who crossed the border, which violated due process rights and negatively affected families and asylum seekers. Ultimately, the "zero-tolerance" policy has resulted in the prosecution of more families, leading to an unprecedented number of families being separated.

In order to protect the nation amidst an era of increased terrorist attacks against the innocent, a global refugee crisis, and the U.S. fighting to maintain its own internal social balance, there must be uniform regulations and procedures at all ports of entry. However, these regulations have to be created with a bi-partisan, inclusive approach and implemented responsibly, without a discriminatory intent.

The family separation policy and the poor treatment of families coming to the U.S. has generated considerable public attention and outrage. The "zero-tolerance" policy underlying this crisis and the abuses accompanying mass criminal prosecutions of immigrants, however, has received less attention.

Although this is the first time a "zero-tolerance" policy resulted in immediate separation of parents traveling with children, this is not the first time the U.S. government has sought to ramp-up criminal prosecution of immigrants. Human Rights Watch research into the history of criminal immigration prosecutions in the U.S. found serious human rights problems, even when families were not being separated at the border. The U.S. government's latest steps to further restrict eligibility for asylum, as well as its stated goal to prosecute 100 percent of those entering illegally, have compounded this harm.

CHAPTER NINE

THE BORDER WALL: HOW CROSSING THE BORDER BECAME A CRIME

The common narrative that most immigrants share about their journey to the United States is that they would do whatever it takes to get here. The promise of hope and opportunity far outweighs any risk involved. Hope is a currency that is endless within the hearts and souls of immigrants because it is one human asset that we can control. Hope isn't determined by race, religion, gender or social class. Hope is an asset that immigrants can control and believe is the bridge to a reality of opportunity. Linda, in her last meeting before we went to court, told me that when her family was making their journey to the U.S., she didn't want to leave Guatemala because she thought she would never see her friends again. She shared that when she asked her parents why they had to leave, her father would always respond that he would be able to give her a better life and keep her safe. He also promised her the bicycle she had always wanted.

History repeatedly evidences the lengths and extremes that immigrants go through to enter this country, including vigorous educational tests, sporting requirements, lotteries and the mercy of makeshift boats where mortal danger is a worthy trade off. This is a reality that most Americans cannot fully comprehend and quite frankly, have no reason to appreciate, because their reality has always been America.

Since 2016, the spotlight has turned to Mexico and the immigration issues at the Mexican border. Ironically, little attention has been given to the history behind the criminalization of illegal entry. Few people realize that prior to 1929, it wasn't a criminal offense to cross the U.S. border without documentation (more on that later).

Yes, there are immigration issues at the border that need to be addressed with a modernized approach and uniform immigration reform. However, based on the Trump administration's narrative, the situation is dire, and the nation's security is in jeopardy because of the "border crisis."

I agree that criminal activity at any border or city needs to be addressed with rule of law to protect the nation. However, the solution has to be relative to the problem. According to U.S. Customs and Border Protection, border crossings have been declining for the last 20 years and are close to an all-time low in modern history. Furthermore, The Migration Policy Institute reports that just 7% of undocumented individuals in the U.S. actually have criminal records. Statistically speaking, 93% of this undocumented population are not violent or felony offenders. So where is the crisis?

My growing concern with a border wall is not the so-called purpose, but its symbolic effect. This strategy was pursued despite statistics showing that illegal border crossings have declined due to technology and better policing. The current polarization of a physical barrier defying statistical logic will perpetuate the ideology that physical separation and force is the solution for keeping out a category of people. Not only will this wall will cost American taxpayers unnecessary spending, but as most failed immigration acts, it will also increase illegal immigration. If an immigrant is willing to die with the hope of coming to the United States, do you really think a wall will stop them? The security of the U.S. borders can be best achieved through bi-partisan guidance, modern technology and trained border agents. Hope is not a weapon used to invade a country.

CHAPTER TEN

THE IMMIGRANT PLAYBOOK: AMERICA'S HISTORY OF IMMIGRANT LABOR AND POLICY

History should have taught us that a broad application of keeping people out of a country based on race, religion and national origin has never solved any national problems. In fact, the opposite occurred -- world and civil wars. The perfect stage has now been set for me to state that the only time people have been let into this country based on their race and national origin (and for the record, the country grew and prospered in every sense) is when people were let in against their will.

With the exception of European immigrants, immigration in the U.S. did not start with people voluntarily coming to this country. Many immigrants, such as Asians, Mexicans and Africans, were recruited or brought to the U.S. involuntarily (nicely put) to satisfy a labor need. Historically, for better or worse, the U.S. has always prioritized its economy.

The Chinese Immigrant Labor Era

In the early 1800's, Mexican immigrants were recruited to the U.S. as laborers for the agriculture, mining and railroad industries. However, it must be noted that the Chinese were the original go-to labor recruits. As history repeats itself, after the need for Chinese labor declined in the post-Civil War economy, guess what? The Chinese became politically demonized and blamed for depressed wages, despite providing low-cost labor to American businesses, paying taxes and not using government infrastructure. State newspapers referred to Chinese immigration as the "Chinese Invasion." Does any of this sound familiar? As a result, in 1882, the Chinese Exclusion Act was born. Generally, this law prohibited all Chinese labor immigration.

The Chinese Exclusion Act was followed by the "driving out" phase. This period saw anti-Chinese Americans physically forced to flee. The increase of violence toward the Chinese included the Rock Spring and Hells Canyon massacres in 1885 and 1887, respectively. Thousands of Chinese immigrants were murdered, tortured and victimized. Why? Because America was done playing with its immigrant toys.

The Need for Mexican Labor

In 1900, recruitment of Mexican laborers skyrocketed due to American railway companies struggling to fill their labor needs. As just discussed, Chinese immigrants were the original go-to laborers, but the Chinese Exclusion Act of 1882 prohibited Chinese labor immigration to the United States. In 1902, Mexican labor was again called on after the passing of the Newlands Reclamation Act. This act lead to an increase in the demand for laborers to help farm more land in the U.S.

As the U.S. economy began to grow and Americans realized that Mexicans were great laborers in the agriculture, railroad, steel and service industries, U.S. businesses and industries recruited and relied heavily on Mexican labor. In case you missed it, there is always a need for non-American laborers because for some reason, Americans either do not fulfill the demand for labor needs or they are not doing a good job at the required positions.

As Mexican labor increased, so did complaints of labor rights abuse amongst Mexican workers, leading to intervention by the Mexican government through creation of a contract to secure Mexican labor rights in the U.S. It required U.S. ranchers to allow Mexican workers to bring their families with them during the contract period. Furthermore, no Mexican worker was allowed to leave for the U.S. without a contract, signed by an immigration official, that stated the rate of pay, work schedule, place of employment and other similar conditions.

The Mexican Labor Debate

As Mexican immigration began to surge, the U.S. and anti-immigration Americans began to complain, resulting in Congress making attempts to limit Mexican labor immigration. Coincidentally or not, Americans did not protest labor immigration from Northern and Western Europe. We can debate and say that Chinese and Mexican immigration was larger than the European labor base, but please don't forget that it was American employers that invited and recruited Mexicans and Chinese to come here for labor.

The irony of the Mexican immigration debate is that when Congress tried to cap Mexican laborers, Southern employers objected. The 1920's saw Western farms becoming completely dependent on Mexican labor. Agriculture was booming and made a significant contribution to the U.S. economy. However, as any reasonable person might expect, the increased reliance on Mexican Labor led to an increase in Mexicans settling in the U.S. Immigrants don't see themselves as temporary or disposable, but non-immigrants tend to differ. Mexicans began building homes, churches and businesses. There is a trade-off for relying on the sweat of immigrants, and the tradeoff is the creation of a culture.

The growing Mexican border culture brought an increase in negative side effects, including illegal border crossings. Immigrants see their sweat as a trade-off for hope and opportunity. Legal border crossing required an entry fee along with literary and health tests. The argument can be made that outside of the demand for Mexican labor, the increase in illegal Mexican border crossings stemmed from the treatment of Mexicans laborers at the ports of entries.

U.S. authorities at the border were notorious for subjecting Mexican laborers to kerosene baths and humiliating delousing procedures because they believed Mexican immigrants carried diseases. Delousing procedures required Mexicans to strip completely naked before a customs inspector. Their clothes were then sterilized in a steam dryer and fumigated with hydrocyanic acid. The customs inspectors also performed lice checks of the scalp, armpits, chest and genital areas. If lice were detected, the inspector would then shave the immigrants' heads and body hair with clippers and require them to bathe with kerosene and vinegar on site.

Some Mexican laborers were who entered the U.S. on a weekly basis had to endure these harsh procedures every single week. In 1921, the U.S. Public Health Service created on-site quarantine and disinfecting sites. It still amazes me that there was no foresight to predict the dangers of bathing humans at kerosene oil sites. In 1916, in the El Paso city jail, someone struck a match near a tub during the mayor's disinfection campaign, and 27 prisoners tragically burned to death.

How Border Crossing Became a Crime

As the Mexican labor debate continued, Congress and American citizens began pushing for restrictions on Mexican labor. Conversely, ranchers and American businesses needed the Mexican labor, and illegal border crossing continued to increase. Then Senator Coleman Blease of South Carolina created a bill and touted that it would solve all of the issues.

The Blease Bill made "unlawfully entering the country" a misdemeanor criminal offense and unlawfully returning to the United States after deportation a criminal felony. Although I am a huge advocate for law and order, the ideology behind this bill directly turned Mexicans into disposable assets that could be controlled at will based on the need of U.S. employers.

It seems as if labor immigration follows a familiar playbook with the ethnic players simply interchanged over time. The game starts with American employers demanding and recruiting foreign labor. The economy thrives on that foreign labor. Then, the demand is reduced, coupled with American workers rebelling against the workers who were recruited to come here. Like clockwork, an act is created to restrict the immigration, and it leads to the labeling, targeting and dehumanization of an ethnic group.

CHAPTER ELEVEN

PROFIT-BASED DETENTION CENTERS

After I graduated from college and was ready to move into working America, I was forced to face my biggest fear -- not the fear of being out of legal immigrant status or being unemployed, but the fear of being detained by Immigration Customs Enforcement (ICE) and deported. At that time, I was transitioning from a student visa to an immigrant visa, which would allow me to legally stay in the country. However, like most immigration change-of-status cases, obstacles were rising and so were the costs.

As an immigrant, you most likely know at least one person who has been detained by ICE and at least three people who have been deported. This fear was very real and frightening for me. The worst part was thinking that I had never committed a crime and was college educated, but my liberty was threatened because of where I was born. The fear of uncertainty and losing the hope that had sustained me since I first came here was daunting. This fear is something every immigrant wakes up with on a daily basis. It is a threatening cloud that persistently hangs over your head -- that you can be detained not for being a criminal, but because you "don't belong."

Immigrant Detention

As I've shared, the inception of the criminalization of border crossing and the increased demand for immigrant labor led to the rise in immigration detention facilities. The immigrant detention system is controlled by several federal agencies. Migrants who are detained as a result of crossing the border are held by Customs and Border Protection (CB) and then eventually transferred to ICE custody. Adults and children traveling together are sent to family detention centers run by ICE. Children traveling alone who can be safely returned to their home countries are deported. If they can't return safely, then they're sent to shelters run by the Office of Refugee Resettlement (ORR). Both CBP and ICE are agencies under the Department of Homeland Security (DHS). The ORR is part of the Department of Health and Human Services.

The majority of detained immigrants are in ICE custody, and the highest number are detained in long-term centers also run by ICE. Reuters revealed in 2018 that ICE reportedly had 41,134 detained immigrants, an increase of more than 10,000 from the previous year. In addition, the Global Detention Project reported that in 2019, 52,000 migrants were held in ICE custody, and 71% of them were detained in privately-operated, for-profit facilities. Because these private prison companies have contracts with the government, they are not required to publicly disclose their agreements. As a result, consumers do not know which companies are working with detainment centers and which ones are not. Based on this information, it is safe to assume that ICE plays a major role in not only governing the detention of immigrants, but also ensuring that the bottom lines of the private detention centers are met.

Before I dive into the growing crisis with immigration detention centers, I must reiterate that these facilities play a role in maintaining law and order in the U.S. and deterring illegal immigration. Just because I am a staunch advocate for immigrants doesn't mean I advocate a free-for-all immigration system where people can enter the U.S. and reap the benefits at will. Not only is that dangerous and reckless, but it's also a slap in the face to immigrants who in many cases, sacrificed everything they had to become legal in the U.S.

If you're in U.S. jurisdiction and you are an immigrant, whether in or out of legal status, and you knowingly commit a crime or worse, become a repeat felony offender, you will be held in a detention facility and likely deported. Most will say this is valid. **However, contrary to popular belief, immigration detention facilities are not primarily made up of immigrants who committed violent crimes, but of immigrants who illegally crossed the border, including asylum applicants, visa over-stayers and misdemeanor offenders.**

Privately-owned Detention Facilities: The Biggest Winners

My biggest issue with the current system is that at least 72 percent of immigrants in detention are being held in privately-owned detention facilities. Anytime I hear "privately owned," I automatically think "for profit," shareholders and a bottom line. When you have a bottom line and profit margins in the same space as human liberty, history has favored profit margins. The years of the Trump administration have revealed the big winners, and I'm pretty sure you can guess who has lost.

Based on reports from the Urban Justice Center's Corrections Accountability project, the two largest companies controlling private detention facilities are GEO Group and CoreCivic, formerly Corrections Corporation of America. In 2017, GEO Group and CoreCivic made a combined $985 million from contracts with ICE. Ladies and gentlemen, these companies are the winners. Again, the problem is when you have a bottom line and profit margins in the same space as human liberty, profit margins will win every time. In this scenario, detained immigrants lose. Because these detention facilities are privately owned and contracted by the government, these companies get paid regardless if the beds are full or not. So arguably, to validate the use of the private facility, government must keep these facilities occupied. In other words, there is an incentive to making sure immigrants are detained. If you're going to have a car payment, you make sure that car is driven, right?

This must be a lucrative business because in 2019, *USA Today* reported that approximately $3 billion a year was spent housing 50,000 detained immigrants. In 2017, revenue reports showed that Geo Group and CoreCivic made close to $4 billion, and their stock value increased by 30 percent. In addition, companies like Bank of America, Wayfair, and American Airlines have all been involved in the business of immigrant detention. This may seem shocking, but it becomes less so when you realize that for-profit migrant detention centers are a multibillion-dollar industry. Chase alone provided a $13 million loan to CoreCivic and gave more than $250 million in revolving credit to both corporations.

Fortunately, public outcry has caused companies like the ones listed above to halt their work with these facilities. Unfortunately, they still exist, and they operate with an alarming amount of secrecy. GEO Group and CoreCivic run the majority of ICE detention facilities. They rely on subcontractors to help their facilities operate, but these vendors are never publicly disclosed. As a result, the industry has been able to grow with little oversight, and some smaller companies are practically untraceable due to their sheer amount of private deals. In 2019, CoreCivic and GEO Group made $4.1 billion between themselves, 25 percent of which came from migrant detention contracts. With money like this on the line, it's no surprise that these mega-corporations are influencing immigration policy changes.

In addition, to preserve profits, corporate lobbyists make huge contributions to political candidates who support their financial interests, which unsurprisingly, include migrant detention. In 2018, CoreCivic spent $1.6 million, and GEO Group spent $2.8 million on funds to support Republican candidates. These types of "donations" encourage an unprecedented expansion of migrant detention. Even if the federal government wanted to expand this dramatically on their own, says ACLU Project Director David Faithi, they would not have the accommodations to do so without the "services" of the private prison industry.

Perhaps the most mind-blowing statistic is that a majority of the detained immigrants had no criminal record. Unfortunately, due to the Trump effect, there has been an increase in immigration restrictions and immigrant detention. Remember, immigration proceedings are labeled as civil proceedings, despite liberty being the currency. Speaking of currency and liberty, Geo Group and CoreCivic contributed hundreds of thousands of dollars toward the 2016 Trump inauguration. I guess they know a good businessman when they see one.

The Biggest Losers

As history has taught us from the immigration playbook, when immigrants are needed and brought to the U.S., the result is economic gain, closely followed by a rebellion from Americans either physically or through policy change. Then comes the grand finale -- a group of people is labeled, abused and victimized.

A 2019 *USA Today* investigation revealed that the standards immigrants have been subjected to in the privately-owned, for-profit detention facilities are less than humane at best. The investigation reported more than 400 allegations of sexual assault or abuse, more than 800 instances of physical force against detainees, regular hunger strikes, inadequate medical care and at least 29 fatalities since 2017. Again, most of the detainees had no criminal convictions.

CHAPTER TWELVE

IMMIGRATION AND THE IMPACT OF COVID-19

As the U.S. and the rest of the world began to grapple with the COVID-19 pandemic in early 2020, the sentiment of "staying home together to save lives" was heard all around the country. The valiant effort and sacrifices by our country's frontline heroes has been an American storyline for which we all became grateful. Nonetheless, despite the tragic loss of life and health to many people in the U.S., the immigrant assault was not suspended.

ICE's fatal response to the COVID-19 crisis caused the virus to unnecessarily claim numerous lives. The pandemic exacerbated and exposed already unregulated and inhumane conditions in the privately-owned detention facilities. The International Rescue Committee reported that over 20 percent of the ICE detained population tested positive in unsanitary and overcrowded ICE facilities. Yet ICE dramatically under-reported COVID-19 cases by a factor of fifteen on average and also failed to release detainees. Once again, keep in mind that the majority of immigrants in these detention centers do not have criminal histories.

The Farmville, Virginia, detention center, run by Immigration Centers of America, boasts a long history of abuse and alleged political spending, and failed immigrants with impunity. According to *The American Prospect*, in August 2020, almost 90 percent of detainees in this facility had tested positive for COVID-19 -- 259 of its 298 residents. This was among the worst in the U.S. for immigration detention centers. Multiple ICA-Farmville detainees have been hospitalized and even more have complained of inadequate medical care. In all, 21 people died in ICE custody at these facilities in 2020, and a third of those deaths were related to the coronavirus.

Despite the atrocities revealed by the COVID-19 pandemic, some of the most restrictive immigration bans came during this time. On March 20, 2020, the Trump administration suspended routine visa services at all U.S. embassies and consulates abroad. Then on April 22, Trump signed the COVID-19 Immigrant Visa Ban that targeted family-based and diversity categories under the disguised purpose of preserving employment opportunities for Americans negatively impacted by the pandemic. The ban reduced immigration into the country. In addition, during this time of economic distress, the Trump administration attempted to increase government filing fees for marriage-based adjustment of status and naturalization applications by almost 60 percent. Luckily, an injunction by a federal judge temporarily halted the fee increase.

Despite the continuous assault, immigrants found a way to be resilient even during a pandemic. The Migration Policy Institute recently reported that six million immigrants are working in frontline occupations such as health care, food production, and transportation. They are also overrepresented in certain critical occupations such as doctors and home health aides, where they face heightened risk of COVID-19 exposure. The Institute further reported that another six million immigrants work in industries that have been economically devastated, such as food services and domestic household services, making up 20 percent of the total workforce in those industries.

Even with the provisions of the $2 trillion Coronavirus Aid, Relief, and Economic Security (CARES) Act and the Pandemic Unemployment Assistance (PUA) program under the CARES Act, many immigrants did not see this benefit. This exacerbated hardships, but the immigrant mindset prevailed. Most immigrants I have interacted with found a way to pivot and to survive. One of my favorite stories is from when I received my first set of masks. They were beautiful, intricately-created, personalized face masks made by a former client whose small food truck business was hit hard by the COVID-19 lockdown. She said she immediately had to come up with a new way to feed her family so she began making masks at her home by hand, with glue and her sewing machine. She has now evolved her business to produce all types of personal protective equipment (PPE) that you can customize with your country's flag or favorite sports team. She found a way!

CHAPTER THIRTEEN

ABOLISH ICE OR REFORM IT?

I met a Nicaraguan girl in 2019. Let's call her Judy. She was happy and playful, but I soon learned that this was the "rehabilitated" version of Judy, which was starkly different from how she had been just three weeks prior. Judy's guardian described to me how Judy was then -- 15 pounds underweight, with her ribs and clavicle visibly protruding. Her hair had blotches missing, and dark circles ringed her eyes. Judy could barely eat because her teeth were black, and her gums were sensitive. She jumped at sudden movements and loud noises.

Judy was six years old when she was taken from her undocumented father during an ICE apprehension. Due to the fact that no other legal guardians could be immediately located, Judy spent weeks in an ICE detention facility until she was released to a guardian. Subsequently, she had to wait to be reunited with a family member in Nicaragua. I was handed a picture of what Judy looked like when she first arrived at the guardian's home, and the tears began streaming down my face.

Judy is the end result when constitutional liberties are no longer afforded to all the "people." An immigration "culture" is created by Americans, but Americans rebel when that culture becomes too large or established. This is then exacerbated when the "culture" can simultaneously become profitable and inhumane. The result is Judy, a loss of innocence and humanity, and the demonization of a group of people.

The Evolution of ICE From Intelligence to Deportation Machine

How did we get here? When did ICE become the flagship of deportation? ICE was established after the September 11, 2001 terrorist attacks. A 2002 *TIME* magazine story stated that the 9/11 terrorist attack was "the biggest intelligence failure in the history of the republic." Even though this is debatable on many levels, I completely agree that an agency needed to be created with the sole purpose of gathering intelligence on potential terrorist threats and eliminating those threats to protect the safety of the American people. However, for some reason, history has shown us that any law, act or agency created within the immigration space skews against immigrants.

During this time, the perception of immigration changed from an economic issue where Americans were deemed to be at an employment disadvantage to a security threat. In 2003, the Department of Homeland Security (DHS) was created as part of one of the government's largest reorganizations. Under the DHS, the U.S. Customs and Border Protection monitors ports of entry, U.S. Citizenship and Immigration Services governs the visa process, and ICE manages detentions and the removal of immigrants who have been previously arrested for immigration violations.

It comes as no surprise that ICE is the DHS' largest investigative weapon. After the devastation of the 9/11 terrorist attacks, the U.S. had to make an equally large response to prevent a recurrence. However, the biggest side effect is that an agency was created to both protect the country from potential national security threats and also to provide a humanitarian approach to handling refugees, asylees, and students who over-stayed their visas. This is tantamount to asking Edward Scissorhands to make balloons at a six-year-old's birthday party -- the intentions are on point, but the execution will be sharp to say the least.

ICE's role is to further the DHS intelligence agenda and enhance public safety by enforcing U.S. federal criminal and civil laws regarding border control, customs, trade and immigration. However, the implementation of ICE represented a major shift in the U.S. approach to immigration.

Previously, immigration matters were handled by the Department of Commerce and then the Department of Labor. This is understandable because the U.S. immigration culture was created due to labor shortages. Conversely, today, immigration is handled by the Department of Homeland Security. This reveals that the U.S. views immigrants as a safety threat. Yes, this is a very generalized and contentious statement, but where is the lie?

Exactly How Do You Get on the ICE Radar?

Currently, there are approximately 10.5 million undocumented immigrants living in the U.S., and according to DHS, in 2017, about one million of the undocumented immigrants have final removal orders. If you have a final removal order, you will be on ICE's radar because that indicates that you enjoyed due process when you were given your notice and the right to be heard by an impartial tribunal.

The obvious route to landing on the ICE radar is if you commit a crime, whether a misdemeanor or felony. However, a felony, where an element of the crime includes violence, theft, a gun or distribution of illegal narcotics, will most likely trigger the ICE radar. In addition, the immigration courts have a different interpretation for state crimes. For instance, an immigrant can be found to be "convicted" of a crime whether they were formally found guilty or not guilty. If there was no official finding of guilt, but the immigrant plead **guilty or no contest ("nolo contendere"),** or if they admit to facts for a finding of guilt to be made and the immigration judge ordered a form of punishment, penalty, payment of court costs, or restraint of liberty, the immigrant in immigration court may be viewed as having been convicted of the crime and deported on that basis. So, an arrest and no conviction may be enough to be on the ICE radar.

An excessive overstay of an expired visa or denied petition, when detected by ICE, is another pathway to landing on the ICE radar. Millions of immigrants either intentionally or unintentionally face the "overstay dilemma." The easiest way to determine an immigrant's length of stay is from their Form I-94 Arrival/Departure Record, which states the date they are expected to leave, and NOT by looking at the length of time since they were issued their visa. Finally, the accrual of unlawful presence that is triggered when there is an overstay can significantly impact an immigrant's ability to reapply, extend their visa and re-enter the country without issues.

Lastly, although not an exhaustive list, an immigrant can find themselves on the ICE radar list and face deportation proceedings by misrepresenting that they are a U.S. citizen or worse, by voting in an election as a U.S. citizen when they're not.

The Conundrum: ICE vs. the U.S. Constitution

Until a purposeful and responsible immigration reform is enacted, immigrants will continue to be mired in the classification of immigration proceedings or infractions being criminal or civil. To the average American, the difference between most civil and criminal proceedings is that you're going to jail or being sued; there isn't a blurred line. As Americans, we feel reasonably safe and empowered when we are home, knowing that the Constitution provides theoretical guidelines that restrict government agencies from entering our homes or searching us without a warrant or probable cause.

In theory, Americans know we can fearlessly file a lawsuit when we feel we have suffered as a result of negligence or a breached contract. We have a right to feel this way because after all, the Constitution is for the people, and it begins with, "We the people." Well, now we are back to "We the people." If you have endured my views to this point, you know that I self-proclaimed that "We the people" refers to all people on U.S. soil, thus entitling all people on U.S. soil to enjoy the protection of the Fourth and Fifth Amendments.

Most immigrants have lived with the overwhelming fear that ICE could come at any moment and take them. This is despite the immigrant knowing that they have never committed a crime against a person or property, that they are a hard worker, and that they pay taxes. However, most immigrants including myself, have come to the sadistic resolve that regardless of how morally whole we are, we can lose our freedom because of our national origin, visa status and label in this country.

The Fourth Amendment of the U.S. Constitution gives, in part, "the right of the people to be secure in their persons, houses, papers, and effects, against unreasonable searches and seizures, shall not be violated, and no warrants shall issue, but upon probable cause…" Now the immigration web begins to tangle because generally, immigration is classified as a civil proceeding. Seemingly, ICE interprets the protections of the Fourth Amendment as inapplicable to immigrants. ICE's apprehension of immigrants through raids and no-warrant entries exposes the vulnerability of immigrants on U.S. soil. There is no recourse or accountability when an immigrant's home is raided or an immigrant is pulled from the streets and detained for simply looking like an immigrant. There is no recourse because unlike criminal court, there is no exculpatory evidence or suppression of evidence as a result of evidence obtained illegally or improperly by law enforcement. There is only deportation. So, ICE is empowered to pursue with minimal government accountability. This is a dangerous space in which to live.

Generally, prisons and jails are viewed as restrictions on liberty as punishment for a criminal offense. However, immigration detention, in theory, is deemed to be preventative in the sense that detention of immigrants during removal proceedings until an immigration judge makes a decision as to whether they will be deported from the country or not, will prevent immigrants from illegally remaining in the country.

The challenge begins because immigrants detained in civil detention don't have to commit, be charged or convicted of a crime to lose their freedom. This issue is exacerbated because so-called civil or immigration detention facilities are run like prisons. I don't know about you, but in my mind, prison only equates to loss of freedom, thus making civil and immigration detention punitive but covered in the gravy of being preventative.

The Supreme Court voiced its thoughts when ruling in several cases that civil detention should be non-punitive in nature. In *Zadvydas v. Davis*, the Court described detention as civil in nature and *"non-punitive in purpose and effect." The Fifth Amendment of the U.S. Constitution protects people against arbitrary denial of liberty by the government. However, immigrants are extremely vulnerable to unlawful imprisonment because, again, ICE operates on the notion that immigrants in deportation proceedings, charged with civil violations, only have civil protection and not protections afforded in the criminal justice system. Civil protection is like using an umbrella in a hurricane.* The constitutional guarantee of due process, and the constitutional guarantee of equal protection and freedom from discrimination based on race, ethnicity, and national origin are rights that are continually taken away from immigrants. I get it. One can argue that these risks are assumed when entering the U.S. as a non-American, but remember, America created the immigration culture, America has economically thrived off the immigrant culture, and therefore, America should be the standard bearer of immigrant culture.

The Benefits of ICE

Clearly, there are many ways to get on the ICE radar, and the method of apprehension may be questionable in a lot of instances. However, don't get me wrong -- ICE has been extremely instrumental in detecting and apprehending child smuggling rings, detecting and ending narcotics smuggling, and getting immigrants who have committed multiple violent felonies off the street. Like any law enforcement agency, ICE is a necessary government tool.

There are immigrants with ill intentions who go against the grain of hope and opportunity. Yes, there are immigrants who commit crimes and unfortunately, crimes against Americans. Yes, there are immigrants who abuse the immigration laws and provide no benefit to the nation or the economy. It is indeed necessary to have an identifiable agency that exclusively investigates a group of people based on their temporary visa status.

It is also necessary to have a defined procedure and process that visa holders such as recruited workers, international professionals and asylum seekers, can be monitored and investigated while on U.S. soil. Finally, it is prudent for any government to confine immigrants if their actions pose a danger to society. Yes, ICE is needed to maintain law and order, even though the statistics show that the benefits of the immigrant culture far outweigh the problems. So how much is ICE really needed?

A government agency such as ICE will only lead to more human rights violations if abolished or defunded. Without any identifiable body, an already targeted and vulnerable class of people would be subject to the mercy of other people who have labeled them as un-American -- not un-American by birth certificate but un-American by perceived value. If ICE is abolished, there will be no accountability process to provide immigrants with what's left of their constitutional rights in U.S. jurisdiction, such as due process. But most importantly, the historical immigrant playbook tells us that without protection, no matter how minimal, when immigrants are labeled and polarized, there will be an increase in mistreatment and hate crimes by American anti-immigrants. **Yes, we need ICE, but we need it to be reformed and its powers kept in check.**

CHAPTER FOURTEEN

MAKE AMERICA GREAT AGAIN

Growing up in the Caribbean in the 90's, if you visited America, shopped in America, studied in America or worked in America, you were the envied "cream of the crop." America was the iconic world leader. This was due in large part to the power of the U.S. Constitution -- a prolific document that outlined an entire government and embedded liberties.

I was in awe of the patriotic right of expression without fear of persecution guaranteed through the First Amendment's freedom of speech. I was wooed by the talent of Hollywood and the drama of American entertainment. I was ready to bet my chances on being my own boss in America with the support of a consistently robust economy, a free market and a capitalistic mindset that is ingrained in the culture. But most importantly, America had lead the way for democracy, liberty and to a certain extent, equality. In my mind, and I'm sure others will agree, America is great and has been great for a very long time!

In 2016, when Trump campaigned on the slogan, "Make America Great Again" (MAGA), it resonated with many Americans. Though MAGA has never been specifically explained or decoded, one can only assume it represents "America First," a sense of patriotic pride, or that it highlighted that

America had a problem that needed to be fixed. Whatever it stood for, enough Americans rallied behind the vision and movement of MAGA to make Trump the 45th President of the United States.

MAGA Wins

In examining MAGA, one cannot deny that under the first three years of the Trump administration, the unemployment rate reached its lowest point in half a century, and 6.7 million jobs were added to the economy. The stock market was hitting record levels, household income grew, poverty decreased, and paychecks grew an average 2.5 percent after inflation.

In addition, Trump historically passed a game-changing tax reform bill, the Tax Cuts and Jobs Act, along with the First Step Act in December 2018. The First Step Act was the first major legislative win in decades to tackle mass incarceration at the federal level, amongst other things. These are a few of the notable wins, and any MAGA supporter will tell you that the MAGA wins are silent because of "fake news" and the constant effort by Democrats to diminish Trump's presidency. Though arguable, it is extremely challenging to deny a consistent recurring narrative of division and a rhetoric of governing some Americans versus all American. Is this what MAGA really represented?

Trump struggled to calm scandals, fueled media whirlwinds and faced high levels of staff turnover within the White House. He became the third president in U.S. history to be impeached. MAGA supporters will vehemently rebut this by saying that the impeachment acquittal evidences a "witch-hunt" by the Democrats and dishonest media. But what about Trump's consistent struggle to lead and serve as a beacon of hope for race relations? What about his frequent inability to denounce white supremacy? Even during Trump's first 2020 presidential debate against former Vice President Joe Biden, when directly asked, Trump could not categorically denounce white supremacy. What am I missing?

The MAGA movement may be a win for domestic optics. However, international relations have significantly declined under Trump. He withdrew the

U.S. from the 2015 nuclear deal in May 2018, arguably creating major issues in the Middle East. The withdrawal was the catalyst to a humanitarian crisis that caused U.S. allies to question their relationship with the U.S. This was followed by the withdrawal from the Paris Climate accord in June 2017 -- an agreement that fulfilled our country's duty as a superpower but conflicted with the MAGA agenda of "America First."

The MAGA movement may deem its biggest win to be curbing illegal immigration. After all, immigration is a platform that illustrates and dramatizes what MAGA represents: "America First," right? I don't know if this is an overall win, because the facts demonstrate that under the Trump administration's watch, the hardline zero tolerance approach led to thousands of immigrant families being separated, children placed in cages, the death of six immigrant children in U.S. custody, numerous human rights abuse violations, and the explosion of immigrant abuse in private detention facilities. Currently, 545 immigrant children cannot find their parents as a result of the 2018 Separation policy. No matter which side of the political aisle you stand, you should be able to objectively recognize what's "America First" versus "America Divided." I wholeheartedly believe that immigration should be a non-political, bipartisan issue -- an oxymoron, I know.

When Has America Ever Been This Great?

So, how did we get here? Was America a broken nation to be made great "again?" Did America need a savior to redeem America's great wealth and global prominence? Was America washed up and yearning to return to its post-World War II, pre-Vietnam "golden years?" Or was MAGA a platform for some Americans who needed to be heard, recognized and elevated?

For starters, Ronald Reagan campaigned on the slogan "Let's make America great again" in 1980. So, MAGA may not be as original as you think. But seriously, what was America being saved from? Does the premise of MAGA want the U.S. to return to the days of segregation before civil rights? Or perhaps the days when women couldn't vote and faced significant disparities in leadership roles and wages, and were viewed solely as child bearers and housewives? Or is MAGA referring to a time period where there were fewer business owners, fewer college graduates and the thought of becoming a millionaire was only something you saw on TV?

In recent times, the United States boasts the most millionaires in the world at 5,671 per 100,000 and the most billionaires in the world at 614 per 100,000, with the next closest being China with 389 billionaires per 100,000. These statistics must count toward some level of success, right? The U.S. saw many glass ceilings shattered by women in the last decade. There has been more diversity in the U.S. in recent times than in any period in U.S. history, from Barack Obama becoming president to Hillary Clinton becoming the Democratic Party nominee. We even saw the first immigrant first lady in the White House in this century (ironically, her last name is Trump). Lastly, immigrant-owned businesses employed almost 8 million American workers and generated $1.3 trillion in total sales. Today, more people in the U.S. have a sense of equality, liberty and peace when compared to other periods in our country's history such as the era of slavery and Jim Crow.

So, I ask the question again, "when has America ever been greater than it is today?" From personal experience as an immigrant, attorney and naturalized citizen, I have witnessed and felt the fibers of American liberties and freedom catapult me to where I am today. Like many of my closest friends, I was able to leverage my American education with American work experience to create the quality of life I envisioned without government infringement or market restrictions. Some may say its luck or that I represent a small percentage of people, but I genuinely feel that America today is one of the very few places where you can be proportionately rewarded for the work and sacrifices that you make.

I have come to the conclusion that initially, MAGA was a representation of the man Donald J. Trump -- a successful marketing campaign. But like other presidents, his presidential term will end, and the man will leave office. The difference with the MAGA era is that when the man leaves, a legacy and the effects of MAGA will remain. However, this time, the impact will not be economic. The transformation of the MAGA platform doesn't see MAGA as solely a presidential platform, but as a foundation for supremacy, division, labeling and marginalization of everything non-American. Under MAGA, the semblance of being non-American has come under siege. Don't get me wrong, the MAGA movement has many people who oppose division and simply want a better economic platform. However, those aren't the loudest voices being heard.

Rise of Xenophobia: The Weaponization of Immigration

I'll be completely honest with you -- I never knew the word xenophobia much less its meaning until Trump came onto the political scene. Per the Merriam-Webster dictionary, xenophobia means the fear and hatred of strangers or foreigners or of anything that is strange or foreign. Coincidentally, in 2016, dictionary.com selected xenophobia as word of the year based on the how the word was trending.

A constant theme throughout this book has been what I call the immigrant playbook and the cyclical culture of immigration. The U.S. created the immigrant culture based on evolving economic needs, which eventually become points of contention for American citizens. Regardless of racial disparities, the U.S. has always represented a melting pot of foreigners. Of course, after the 9/11 terrorist attacks, there was a shift in the way the U.S. government viewed foreigners and immigrants. Immigration switched from an economic concern to a homeland security issue. Arguably, this could be justified.

In 2016, another event altered the perception of immigrants -- the presidential campaign of Donald Trump and the birth of MAGA. "[Mexican illegal immigrants] are bringing drugs. They're bringing crime. They're rapists. And some, I assume, are good people." Sound familiar? The MAGA campaign thrived on labelling immigrants as a threat to American people, but we have seen this before in the immigrant playbook, right? "Immigrant labor is undercutting the job market, reducing wages and causing unemployment amongst Americans." Even though ironically, Trump's restrictions on immigration exacerbated America's labor shortage by ignoring the high demand for unskilled immigrant workers, and yes, even at his own golf clubs.

This narrative has persisted throughout U.S. immigration history since the 1800's. However, the difference now is that immigrants are being labeled as rapists, criminals and a threat to everyday life. These were words uttered and publicized by the President of the United States himself. The Trump campaign and presidency also transformed the meaning of "America First." Whether Trump saw this as an opportunity to resonate with Americans who have always been anti-immigrant or Americans whose perception of "America First" is actually hate or supremacy of anything non-American, this rhetoric has defined the MAGA identity and movement.

MAGA has spawned the birth of xenophobia where immigration and immigrants are now a scapegoat for economic issues and domestic threats despite factual data proving otherwise. Trump has seemingly relied on a xenophobic sentiment to justify his administration's hardline immigration policies. However, in addition to helping him garner a loyal base, the labeling of immigrants in the U.S. and the blatant promotion of xenophobia has resulted in numerous negative consequences, including a significant increase in reported hate crimes from 2016-2020.

The FBI reported that in 2018, personal attacks motivated by bias or prejudice reached a 16-year high, with a significant increase in violence against Latinos. From 2016-2020, there was also an increase in domestic terrorism aimed at racial, ethnic and minorities in the U.S. I can confidently say that when you have the Commander in Chief repeatedly labeling and separating people by their ethnicity, regardless of the overall intent, it will breed negative effects.

This xenophobic rhetoric has also spawned many groups that are "anti-anything not American." The Southern Poverty Law Center stated that the number of hate groups in the United States has risen significantly since 2016, and attributed the record increase in hate crimes to a toxic combination of political polarization, anti-immigrant sentiment and technologies that help spread propaganda online. According to one study, the majority of reported hate crimes since the 2016 election have been concentrated in counties that Trump won by large margins. Data shows that this wave of hate crimes is the largest uptick in the last two and a half decades. Furthermore, the Anti-Defamation League has also released data showing counties that hosted Trump campaign rallies during the 2016 election had double the number of hate crimes when compared to similar counties that didn't hold Trump rallies.

The U.S. has always had a contentious race relations history. Many of the current hate groups existed prior to the MAGA era, and previous administrations have also polarized immigration. However, what is different about the MAGA era is that never in recent history has there been a President of the United States who blatantly governs some Americans versus all Americans and is so cavalier when it comes to denouncing hate groups.

CHAPTER FIFTEEN

IMMIGRANT LIVES MATTER

Change won't come until the "unaffected" identify with the "affected." Most Americans can't and won't comprehend the process of immigration or the effects of being labeled as "immigrant" or worse, "undocumented immigrant." Personally, I have had my share of being labeled. In college, I remember being told that I sailed here on a banana boat. At the time, I laughed it off, but those words stung. I've lost count of the number of times I've been asked for my green card or ID after speaking with my accent. I have witnessed the look of pity on people's faces when I tell them that I grew up in Jamaica, and I will never understand that. As a college athlete, I was frequently told "immigrants should not be allowed to compete in the NCAA." But the words that always cut the deepest are, "go back to where you came from." Even though I pride myself on having tough skin, comments and actions reflecting this mindset can cut deep and are what most immigrants face on a daily basis.

A former client of mine -- I will call her Trisha -- came to the U.S. on a student visa from the Caribbean. Her plan was to return to her home country to pursue a career in civil engineering with her new degree. However, along the way, she was swept off her feet by a man -- a U.S. citizen. Soon after, the couple got married and had a child. This is a very common love story.

However, things took a turn for the worse. Trisha wanted to legally reside in the U.S. and began filing her adjustment of status petition to become a legal permanent resident – a green card holder. After submitting her green card application, Trisha was in a "pending" temporary status until approval. Unfortunately, during this time, her marriage became abusive, and her husband would constantly threaten Trisha with deportation and to cancel the adjustment of status petition and notify ICE.

I explained to Trisha that under no circumstances she should endure physical and mental abuse just to stay in the U.S. She said she was afraid to report the abuse to the police for fear of not being believed because she was an immigrant. She was also scared that her child could be taken from her if she was deported. I continued to encourage Trisha that she was educated and valued, and that there were other options outside of enduring the abuse and being held hostage.

Despite my efforts, Trisha's fear of being deported and seen as "less than" by law enforcement crippled her ability to leave the relationship, and I haven't heard from her since. It is unfortunate that immigrants are good enough to become spouses and good enough to bear American children, but not good enough to be seen as equal because of their national origin. This is a common theme I have encountered while representing immigrants. Nonetheless, we continue to endure and persevere in the name of hope.

It's not the categorizing that affects immigrants the most, it's that feeling of being "less than." It's the feeling that no matter what you achieve or how hard you work, you don't belong. And yes, I get it, some will say, "well, you weren't born here so you're not entitled to be here." My response is, "don't invite us to party if you don't want to dance." America has significantly benefited from immigrant cultures and immigrant contributions. Most importantly, America created the culture of bringing in immigrant labor, talent and love for its own benefit.

Black Lives Matter

The culture of the "unaffected" being unable to identify with the "affected," is the foundation of most race and "labeling" issues in America. In recent years, we have witnessed an increase in black American injustices, and the volume of systemic racism has grown louder. One can argue that statistically, there has not been an increase, only a polarization through social media and the prevalence of smart phones, equipping more people with the ability to record video of injustices than in previous eras. Some will also argue that black America has to take responsibility for their own actions and interactions with law enforcement. Nonetheless, whichever argument you make, it still doesn't account for what black Americans experience simply because of being black in America.

The Black Lives Matter movement is a voice of the "affected," and the inherent privilege of the "unaffected" is evident when "All Lives Matter" is used simultaneously to invalidate the cries of the Black Lives Matter movement. What the "unaffected" don't understand is that the mere action of saying, "All Lives Matter," is the reason why "Black Lives Matter" needs to be said. When black Americans say, "Black Lives Matter," it's not to say black lives matter more than other lives. Instead, it is a voice trying to speak to the "unaffected," the people who can't live the life of a black person or experience the hardships or struggles black people face solely because of the color of their skin. It's the "unaffected's" inability to recognize that they are blind, some consciously and some subconsciously, to the fact that their words and actions significantly minimize and marginalize black people. Black Lives Matter is a hand being raised to alert you that they are in imminent danger or suffering harm. It is the voice of people like George Floyd who tragically died because of someone "unaffected" who did not value his black life.

However, this is not the day for a full court press on the Black Lives Matter movement. The most unfortunate representation of the "unaffected" is the President's classification of the Black Lives Matter movement as a terrorist organization and political issue. You can't stifle a voice more than that.

In my opinion, the MAGA movement has transitioned from a political campaign to a warped version of an "America First" mindset. Remember, Black Lives Matter started as a voice, a platform for protest by the "affected." Now, all of a sudden, the "affected," the distressed voice of a group of people, is labeled as a political group with the only intention of wreaking havoc on America. How did I miss that pivot? I completely understand that the Black Lives Matter movement has evolved into an organization for some. I also see and condemn those who loot, kill and politicize what is meant to be a peaceful protest movement.

Then there is the narrative that the Black Lives Matter movement is synonymous to Antifa and other counter-protesting groups. Antifa (short for "antifascist"), is described as a loose collection of groups, networks and individuals that advocate aggressive opposition to far right-wing movements both online and in real life. If people conducted research before speaking out, they would discover that the missions of Antifa and Black Lives Matter are completely different. One is exclusively political and the other is an advocate for social justice. The most egregious tragedy has been the assumption that once an issue becomes politically driven and Trump co-signs, it is gospel, it is truth, it is MAGA. But the stifling effect remains -- the suppression of the voice of the "affected" once again by the "unaffected."

Immigrants Make America Great

Immigrants in Trump's America face an addition barrier as the "affected." With the MAGA narrative, the polarization of immigration and the increase in xenophobia, immigrants are now raising their hands -- the immigrants who are separated from their families, the immigrants who are subjected to sub-human standards in cages, the immigrants who are judged and marginalized because of their national origin, the immigrant families who are terrified to send their children to school because of bullying, and the immigrants who can't keep a job, not because of their qualification or work ethic, but because they are here on a visa. Again, some of these problems aren't new, but the MAGA movement has made the immigrant more vulnerable than ever before.

Ironically, immigrants are also marginalized and treated as a sub-category of people by some black Americans. The culture of "go back where you came from" is perpetuated by some black Americans because at the end of the day, despite the challenges endured by black people in America, a black American can tell an immigrant to go home. A black American can create barriers for an immigrant in every aspect of life because of the vulnerability of immigrants. This may seem harsh, but as a black immigrant, I can speak from my own personal experience. This proves my point that **change won't come until the "unaffected" identify with the "affected."** Despite the challenges black Americans face, they aren't affected in the same way as immigrants and can't comprehend some of the unique hardships immigrants must endure. It is even more unfortunate that a President of the United States can be culpable for perpetuating the stifling and marginalization of the "affected" just by his words or lack thereof.

The challenges that immigrants share, regardless of their color, are what make them great. The additional barriers of language, cultural assimilation, documented status and marginalization are what generate the resilience that most immigrants share. They are either driven by the fear of returning to their home country or by hope. Their hope shines through in their innate ability to thrive no matter the circumstances. Most immigrants win because the risk of losing far outweighs what they have had to overcome and rise above.

Immigrants Act More as "Job Creators" Than "Job Takers"

I can completely see why over the last three centuries the U.S. has relied heavily on the diversity and skill that immigrants bring to the American labor force and culture. **In 2017, nearly 50 percent of the businesses on the Fortune 500 list of companies were founded by immigrants or their children. In 2020, 40 percent of new companies have an immigrant involved in their founding.** In fact, one in every four entrepreneurs is an immigrant. Entrepreneurship is a quintessential representation of the American culture.

In many industries, immigrant entrepreneurs have blazed trails for innovation. They serve as role models for transferring their unique perspectives and ingenuity into opportunities in the U.S. According to the 2012 *"Open for Business: How Immigrants are Driving Small Business Creation in the United States"* report by New American Economy, **immigrant entrepreneurs contribute to the U.S. annual gross domestic product (GDP) with over $775 billion in revenue.** Let that sink in.

Immigrants have also solidified themselves in American culture. The COVID-19 pandemic really highlighted America's reliance on immigrants. The Migration Policy Institute (MPI) **reported** that 6.3 million immigrants hold jobs that are key to fighting the coronavirus. In the United States, 29% of all physicians are immigrants. In other words, **one in four** doctors in the U.S. **are immigrants.** America is aging, and the elderly are especially vulnerable to COVID-19. Once again, immigrants are called to duty – **38 percent** of home health aides are immigrants. In addition, according to U.S. Census data, nearly a third of agricultural workers nationwide are foreign-born. Without counting those who are undocumented, **22 percent** of **workers in the U.S. food industry are immigrants**, and **35 percent of crop production workers are immigrants. According to MPI,** around 16% of America's approximately three million grocery retail workers **are immigrants. Statistically, that means 483,000 immigrants work in grocery stores. I could share statistics all day, but let's get more granular as to how immigrants play huge roles in American culture.**

What do Google, eBay, WhatsApp, Instagram and thousands of other successful companies have in common? They were each founded by an immigrant entrepreneur. Sergey Brin escaped the former Soviet Union to come to America and later co-founded Google. Yes, the Google. Jan Koum fled persecution in Ukraine as a teenager, paving the way for him to become the founder of WhatsApp. Pierre Omidyar, born in Paris to Iranian immigrant parents, immigrated to the U.S. and created eBay. Mike Krieger, a Brazilian tech entrepreneur, co-founded Instagram. Furthermore, according to a new National Foundation for American Policy (NFAP) analysis, foreign-born players make up 23 percent of the rosters in the National Basketball Association (NBA), 29 percent in Major League Baseball (MLB) and 72 percent in the National Hockey League (NHL).

So, immigrants not only raise the level of innovation in the U.S. and create jobs, they also positively impact the quality of sports, sports revenue and the consumer experience. History has unequivocally evidenced the fall of American innovation when immigration is restricted. In the 1920's, immigration quotas caused a significant decline in American innovation in part because Americans were less innovative without the presence and diversity of immigrants.

Whether its eating at your favorite ethnic restaurant, watching your favorite sports team or getting your yard cut, immigrants represent more than what MAGA believes. It is an injustice to let Trump and the MAGA movement politicize and dictate to America that the word "immigrant" captures only Latinos or Mexicans at the border. We must not let MAGA create a culture of marginalizing, labeling and then degrading a group of people just because they weren't born here. Immigrant lives matter.

CHAPTER SIXTEEN

THRIVING AND WINNING IN AMERICA

I heavily relied on diligence and determination to navigate the immigration waters of the U.S. Though I was denied a couple of times before receiving my legal permanent resident status, I knew I had to keep pushing. I knew the visions of success I had as a teenager would come to fruition. I believed this because America rewards hard work, America gives second chances, and America loves a great comeback story. I have thrived on these three tenets. Most immigrants share a similar journey and have depended upon their diligence and determination. As immigration is under siege and immigrants become more vulnerable than ever before, we will rise to the occasion and not only survive, but thrive.

Protect Yourself

During the Trump administration, we witnessed sweeping changes to the U.S. immigration laws -- from the growing travel ban list to increased scrutiny when filing visa applications and petitions to higher filing fees and additional caps on employment visas. In my practice, I have noticed that USCIS is denying more applications and petitions. The burden of proof for immigrants has significantly increased for applications and petitions to be approved.

It is evident that the restrictionist approach has been in full effect while Trump is President and potentially will continue for years after. Yes, I can say that some of these policies are being enforced as a matter of national security, and some of the changes are necessary to streamline immigration. However, Trump's immigration overhaul and the optics it created were primarily to appeal to MAGA.

> "We're not a nation that kicks out strivers and dreamers who want to earn their piece of the American Dream. We're a nation that finds a way to welcome them. We make them earn it, but we welcome them in as fellow human beings, fellow children of God. And we harness their talents to make the future brighter for everybody."
>
> — President Barack Obama, November 21, 2014

Trump's 2020 agenda to reduce legal immigration most harms refugees, employers and Americans who want to live with their spouses, parents or children, but it also affects the country's future labor force and economic growth. With these clouds looming overhead, immigrants in the U.S. and immigrants planning to come to the U.S. must protect themselves.

I believe that like myself, most immigrants strive for the American Dream of life, liberty and the pursuit of happiness. In that same breath, I hold immigrants accountable. I believe that as immigrants, we do not have a birthright to anything in the U.S.; however, we should be able to earn that right. As humans, we are born with innate talents and passions, that when combined, can make our potential limitless. However, while in the U.S., we must follow the baseline rules to provide ourselves that opportunity of pursuing the American Dream. Here are my five primary rules for immigrants:

1. **Do not overstay your visa.** This may be difficult for immigrants with exigent circumstances. However, if this can be avoided, it should because the potential avenues and immigration advantages are significantly reduced when an immigrant overstays

their visa. Immigrants should research and know the terms and requirement of their visas as well as how to transition from a visa to permanent residence if that's a goal.

2. **If you are concerned about potential interaction with ICE, always carry immigration documentation.** In addition, if you are subject to an ICE raid, do not allow ICE in your home without proof of a federally signed warrant. Also, do not sign any documentation provided by ICE without a first talking to an attorney. I've had so many clients sign away substantive rights because they did not understand what they were signing or felt pressured to sign. If all else fails, shut up!

3. **Don't commit a crime.** Whether it's a misdemeanor or felony, committing a crime hurts immigrants significantly more than it does U.S. citizens. If you are an immigrant and get arrested, not only will your liberty be taken away, but you are potentially exposed to deportation, depending on the crime. My mother always told me, "when you go to someone's house, you must take better care of it than your own." This is a value I live by and is a mindset I believe immigrants should adopt. If you weren't born here, you should follow all the rules and even go above and beyond to legally and ethically achieve your dreams and goals.

4. **Develop a plan.** I've learned that most goals in life are achieved by a having plan that has been carefully executed. When I was 16 years old, I mapped out how I wanted to pursue my American Dream. I knew I had to train to run fast and earn specific grades to be eligible to get recruited by an American college. I understand that most immigrants' situations are different than mine, and some are genuinely trying to escape persecution. However, researching and strategizing your immigration plan to the U.S. takes thought, time, money and hardship. Complex situations

will require professional help, but educating yourself before even entering the country will create significant advantages.

5. **Add value.** This may be listed last, but it certainly is not least. Determine how you will add value to the American economy and culture.

6. **Thrive!**

There is a reason why despite all of the legal changes, xenophobia and obstacles to immigration, people still flock to the U.S., immigrants still fight to stay in this country, and I am still here on my soapbox: **The United States of America still provides the most opportunities to pursue Life, Liberty and Happiness.** Regardless of which administration is in power, which immigration law Trump reversed or how the MAGA nation feels about immigrants, we will find a way to thrive.

How Immigrants Can Add Value

In navigating all of the noise, immigration policies aside, immigrants must find a way to capitalize on the current landscape. The undeniable trait to succeed in the U.S. today is to add value by being more qualified, more skilled, more experienced and more versatile in all endeavors. As immigrants, adding value must be our daily currency. U.S. citizens recognize this approach, and it can be an economic equalizer, no matter where you are from.

As an immigrant coming to the U.S. or living here, being more qualified will always provide a springboard to greater career opportunities. This includes scholarships, higher-paying jobs and sponsorship from a company for an employment visa. Immigrants possess the ability to add a unique perspective to problem-solving and innovation. These are traits that we all can capitalize on, even in Trump's economy.

The Trump era has promoted economic freedom through major deregulatory actions. Deregulation removes or reduces state regulation with the goal of making it easier to do business. MAGA will continue to complain about immigrants and socially attack us. However, with Trump's love for private markets and creating lower barriers to conducting business, there are opportunities for immigrants to capitalize. Free or private markets thrive on innovation, competition and increased consumer choice, and a valued immigrant provides just that.

So, if there is an opportunity to obtain a degree, a certification or specialty, do it. Many colleges and workplaces love checking the "diversity box." So, apply for that position, program or school. In an economy that is saturated with private business, companies will overlook visa status for value.

Real Estate

The more things change, the more they stay the same. It is an old cliché, but it's true. Real estate is and will always be a consistent tool to acquiring stability. Most immigrants get caught up in the daily rat race just to survive. Whether you're a temporary visa holder, green card holder or transitioning your legal status, real estate ownership should be in your strategy. According to the Migration Policy Institute, in 2014, approximately 3.4 million undocumented immigrants owned homes. That is roughly 31 percent or almost a third of the U.S. undocumented population. In addition, the Institute on Taxation and Economic policy reported in 2017 that undocumented immigrants had contributed as much as $3.6 billion in property taxes alone. This is a starkly different tale than what MAGA promotes.

ITIN Mortgage

Yes, resources are required to buy a home. However, immigrants underestimate their strength in unity. The Jewish and Chinese communities are prime examples of combining their resources to secure a future. For example, Chinese immigrants show their strength in numbers through their closely-knit communities, by supporting their native businesses, and by transferring their knowledge, business acumen and resources from generation to generation. Furthermore, legal status is not required to own property in the U.S. An investment tool known as an ITIN mortgage can help you start a journey toward land ownership. ITIN stands for individual tax identification number and is an alternative to a Social Security number that enables foreign nationals who own businesses or property in the U.S. to pay taxes on these assets. This is available to all immigrants, regardless of status. ITIN also allows documented and undocumented immigrants the ability to open bank accounts, pay income taxes and potentially qualify for a mortgage on a home. Yes, there are more details and procedures, but this is a great starting point for your pursuit of the American Dream.

Under the Trump administration, the Treasury and Housing and Urban Development departments have revealed housing plans with the goal to end government control of Fannie Mae and Freddie Mac. These two entities control half of all U.S. mortgages. If Trump's goal is to open the housing market to allow more competition with private companies, this also allows immigrants greater opportunities to own real estate as well as additional opportunities for immigrants and immigrant communities to pool resources and create a better platform for immigrant stability and generational growth.

Business Ownership

Whether documented or undocumented, one common theme for immigrants is the "find a way" mindset. It is the belief that, "if I can't work or if I won't get hired, I will find a way." This was my thought process when I entered the job market after earning both a bachelor's degree and MBA in college. I was determined to find a way. However, after sending out over 100 resumes and participating in countless interviews, I was left unsatisfied. Even after earning my law degree and passing the Florida Bar, I still faced barriers to employment. I remember putting on my very best suit, walking into corporate buildings to drop off resumes to law firms, and trying to talk my way into speaking with the law partners. Most of my efforts proved futile. After finally getting lucky and working for two different law firms, with mixed experiences, I still wanted to find my own way. So, I proudly started my own law firm with no loans or equity partners -- just hard work, sweat equity and the will to find a way.

My story isn't unique by any means -- it is a story shared by many immigrants. In fact, U.S. Census Bureau statistics indicate the following:

1. Immigrants are nearly twice as likely to start businesses compared to American-born citizens. In fact, as many as eight to 10 percent of undocumented immigrants own businesses.

2. Business formation rates are even higher among immigrants than non-immigrants.

3. Immigrant-owned businesses are slightly more likely to hire employees than are non-immigrant-owned businesses.

4. 4mmigrant-owned businesses are more likely to export their goods and services than are non-immigrant-owned businesses.

Regardless of your immigration status, you are able to start a business in the U.S. Don't get me wrong, it won't absolve you from deportation if pursued by ICE, and immigrants must always prioritize legally staying in the U.S. However, that's not always the case, and government regulators, banks and institutional lenders provide opportunities for business owners regardless of their visa status. And in some cases, owning a business is a factor that can help to prevent deportation.

Even under Trump's rule, immigrants can maximize business ownership. The only thing Trump has pushed more than immigration is the economy. I must confess that before Trump went on his immigrant-bashing escapade, I enjoyed the thought of a businessman running the country because the best business owners find a way. In my mind, this could be a win for immigrants. But little did I know that the trade-off for a businessman running the country would be zero soft skills and relatability when it comes to immigrants.

Under Trump, there has been a push for "opportunity zones" that incentivize private investment into marginalized communities. Coupled with generous corporate tax cuts and favorable business benefits, these are opportunities on which immigrants can capitalize. No, immigrants more likely than not won't pay only $750 in federal income taxes, but there are encouraging opportunities for immigrant business owners. Again, immigrants must pool assets, talent resources and capital to maximize every opportunity America has to offer. Trump's America has proven that America will choose a robust economy and open labor force over social issues. Since we as immigrants can't change that narrative, we must learn to thrive off of it.

Immigrants also bring culture to the U.S. that is continuously monetized, including restaurants, entertainment and innovation. Immigrants must acknowledge this as a part of our value and use it as a weapon to thrive. Culture, ingenuity and competition are the hallmarks of immigrant businesses and immigrant entrepreneurs. We must own this rhetoric, irrespective of MAGA, because when all is said and done, America feeds on immigrant culture way more than immigrants feed off of America.

Building Community

The most underrated tool immigrants have at their disposal is community. My definition of community is when a group of people live out the saying, "each one reach one, each one, teach one." The ability for a younger person to have a tangible representation of success is integral to any group evolving. In addition, the lessons learned along the road to success are an asset that should be shared amongst all immigrants. This isn't a unique theory, but it is grossly overlooked.

A game-changing moment for me was in my early 20's when my path crossed with two successful immigrant men -- a Jamaican doctor and a French real estate investor. Their words, but more importantly, witnessing their lives, completely changed my perspective and elevated the ceiling for what I once thought an immigrant could achieve.

I am fortunate to come from a family of hard workers -- both of my parents were teachers, and they instilled in me the importance of education, a strong work ethic and self-respect. The difference that the Jamaican and Frenchman made for me was they shared their journeys as immigrants in the U.S. They had similar storylines of vision and execution. The Jamaican solidified in my mind that someone from my country can use education, skill and resilience to gain success. He shared his mistakes and his roadmap, which I could relate to, identify and embody. The Frenchman shared with me his business acumen and his network, and he helped me appreciate the value of strategized risk. Without these two immigrants with starkly different immigrant journeys sharing their roadmaps and experiences, I would not have had tangible and relatable examples of how to use my unique tools as an immigrant to achieve success in America. "Each one, reach one" -- every immigrant, whether family or stranger, should strive to share their journey in navigating the U.S. waters. "Each one, teach one" -- consistent, deliberate mentorship in immigrant communities will make a difference in the leadership within the immigrant community. America will only value our contributions once we add value and value ourselves.

The Immigrant Mind

Though I was not born in this country, I always had the American Dream. This wasn't because I didn't love my country, but because I knew my country equipped me with tools and skills to fight for my dream anywhere. My intent, and that of most immigrants who come to the U.S., is to prosper economically, add to the American labor force and achieve freedom of self-expression without government interference.

The baseless narrative that immigrants come to the U.S. to change or wreak havoc on American democracy and values couldn't be further from the truth. Most immigrants fight to succeed in the U.S. because they value family -- a value that is a fundamental ingredient in the U.S. Constitution and American culture. We come here embracing American culture because we believe in the protection of family that it provides. We fight for this culture -- whether it's on the front line to defend the U.S. or on the front line to fight a pandemic -- because we want to protect the American Dream, our dream. Immigration transcends political party lines and should be a unified humanitarian fight with bipartisan economic advocates.

The suffering and struggles in most immigrants' home countries are actually an advantage that we bring with us to America. We have the asset of knowing what hardship truly is, and we hold a clear view of what the bottom really looks like. We also know that we will not take America for granted or expect a handout to gain the American Dream. The reality is that for most immigrants, it is the quest to achieve the American Dream that outweighs any obstacle, wall or mortal danger we must face to get here.

America promises a dream in which immigrants strongly believe -- a dream to "we the people." It's a dream that most immigrants can't avoid. American history and culture have been enriched by immigrants. It is impossible to narrate U.S. history without stories of immigrants. This is a culture that America's Founding Fathers created by inviting and opening the U.S. borders to the rest of world.

Yes, the world today is not what it used to be, and America looks completely different than it did a century ago. But America has not become weaker because it became different; America became stronger because it embraced the differences. Yes, a rule of law is required and must be uniformly implemented. However, the rule of law should not seek to exclude or be implemented by fear against the ingredient that has made America great – immigrants.

My life is a representation of the American Dream. The process of realizing this dream, like anything worth fighting for, was difficult and tantamount to an obstacle course where progression is rewarded by another obstacle. The MAGA mindset runs contrary to the fundamental origins and values of America. The xenophobia and disdain toward immigrants is ironic since most Americans are descendants of immigrants, who like me, had to work hard and battle to achieve the American Dream. Today, the fight is compounded by the polarized narrative that immigrants are second-class citizens, invading and robbing Americans of opportunities and culture. But like every period in U.S. history, we will evolve, we will adapt, and we will find a way. But most importantly, we will thrive.

REFERENCES

Chapter One

Roy Germano, "Unauthorized Immigrants Paid $100 Billion Into Social
Security Over Last Decade," *Vice,* August 4, 2014. https://www.vice.
com/en/article/zm5k8j/unauthorized-immigrants-paid-100-billion-
into-social-security-over-last-decade

Chapter Two

"Immigrant-Owned Businesses Employed 8 Million Americans;
Immigrants Wield $1.1 Trillion in Spending Power," New American
Economy, March 12, 2019. https://www.newamericaneconomy.
org/press-release/new-data-shows-immigrant-owned-businesses-
employed-8-million-americans-immigrants-wield-1-1-trillion-in-
spending-power/

President Donald J. Trump's State of the Union Address, Issued on:
January 30, 2018. https://www.whitehouse.gov/briefings-statements/
president-donald-j-trumps-state-union-address/

Julia Gelatt and Sarah Pierce, "The Trump Immigration
Plan: A Lopsided Proposal," Migration Policy Institute,

January 2018. https://www.migrationpolicy.org/news/
trump-immigration-plan-lopsided-proposal

H.R.1044 - Fairness for High-Skilled Immigrants Act of 2019. https://www.
congress.gov/bill/116th-congress/house-bill/1044

Chapter Three

Convention Relating to the Status of Refugees, Adopted on July 28,
1951, by the United Nations Conference of Plenipotentiaries on the
Status of Refugees and Stateless Persons. https://www.ohchr.org/en/
professionalinterest/pages/statusofrefugees.aspx

Refugee Act of 1980. https://www.archivesfoundation.org/documents/
refugee-act-1980/

"USCIS to Take Action to Address Asylum Backlog, U.S. Citizenship and
Immigration Services," January 30, 2018. https://www.uscis.gov/
uscis-to-take-action-to-address-asylum-backlog

Procedures for Asylum and Withholding of Removal; Credible Fear
and Reasonable Fear Review. A Proposed Rule by the Homeland
Security Department and the Executive Office for Immigration
Review on 06/15/2020. https://www.federalregister.gov/
documents/2020/06/15/2020-12575/procedures-for-asylum-and-
withholding-of-removal-credible-fear-and-reasonable-fear-review

Deferred Action for Childhood Arrivals (DACA), U.S. Department of
Homeland Security, June 15, 2012. https://www.dhs.gov/xlibrary/
assets/s1-exercising-prosecutorial-discretion-individuals-who-came-
to-us-as-children.pdf

Chapter Four

Article 1, Section 8, U.S. Constitution. https://constitutioncenter.org/interactive-constitution/article/article-i

Nationality Act of 1790. https://immigrationhistory.org/item/1790-nationality-act/

Chinese Exclusion Act. https://guides.loc.gov/chinese-exclusion-act

Immigration Act of 1891. https://www.loc.gov/law/help/statutes-at-large/51st-congress/session-2/c51s2ch551.pdf

Immigration Act of 1924. https://history.house.gov/Historical-Highlights/1901-1950/The-Immigration-Act-of-1924/

1966 Cuban Refugee Adjustment. https://www.govinfo.gov/content/pkg/STATUTE-80/pdf/STATUTE-80-Pg1161.pdf

Refugee Act of 1980. https://www.govinfo.gov/content/pkg/STATUTE-94/pdf/STATUTE-94-Pg102.pdf

Deferred Action for Childhood Arrivals (DACA), U.S. Department of Homeland Security, June 15, 2012. https://www.dhs.gov/xlibrary/assets/s1-exercising-prosecutorial-discretion-individuals-who-came-to-us-as-children.pdf

Chapter Five

U.S. Bill of Rights. https://www.archives.gov/founding-docs/bill-of-rights-transcript

Fourteenth Amendment, U.S. Constitution. https://constitutioncenter.org/interactive-constitution/amendment/amendment-xiv

Second Amendment, U.S. Constitution. https://constitutioncenter.org/interactive-constitution/amendment/amendment-ii

Fourth Amendment, U.S. Constitution. https://constitutioncenter.org/interactive-constitution/amendment/amendment-iv

Ninth Amendment, U.S. Constitution. https://constitutioncenter.org/interactive-constitution/amendment/amendment-ix

Tenth Amendment, U.S. Constitution. https://constitutioncenter.org/interactive-constitution/amendment/amendment-x

Associated Press, "Grand Rapids to Pay $190K to Latino US Citizen Held by ICE," November 13, 2019. https://apnews.com/article/4de6e90d3fea4d0db30e6254a6b600de

Fifth Amendment, U.S. Constitution. https://constitutioncenter.org/interactive-constitution/amendment/amendment-v

Designating Aliens for Expedited Removal: A Notice by the Homeland Security Department on 07/23/2019. https://www.federalregister.gov/documents/2019/07/23/2019-15710/designating-aliens-for-expedited-removal

Reno v. Flores, 507 U.S. 292 (1993). https://supreme.justia.com/cases/federal/us/507/292/

Sixth Amendment, U.S. Constitution. https://constitutioncenter.org/interactive-constitution/amendment/amendment-vi

Gideon v. Wainwright, 1963 https://www.uscourts.gov/educational-resources/educational-activities/facts-and-case-summary-gideon-v-wainwright

Plyler vs. Doe, 457 U.S. 202 (1982). https://www.uscourts.gov/educational-resources/educational-activities/access-education-rule-law

Chapter Six

Meyer v. State of Nebraska, 262 U.S. 390 (1923). https://www.loc.gov/item/usrep262390/

Pierce, Governor of Oregon, et al. v. Society of the Sisters of the Holy Names of Jesus and Mary and Hill Military Academy, 268 U.S. 510 (1925). https://www.law.cornell.edu/supremecourt/text/268/510

Chapter Seven

"New Americans in Longview, Texas," New American Economy, May 12, 2020. https://research.newamericaneconomy.org/report/new-americans-in-longview-texas/

Attorney General Announces Zero-Tolerance Policy for Criminal Illegal Entry. https://www.justice.gov/opa/pr/attorney-general-announces-zero-tolerance-policy-criminal-illegal-entry

Robert Warren, "Overstays Exceeded Illegal Border Crossers after 2010 Because Illegal Entries Dropped to Their Lowest Level in Decades," Center for Migration Studies. https://cmsny.org/publications/essay-warren-042419/

Chapter Eight

HHS OIG Issue Brief, January 2019, OEI-BL-18-00511, "Separated Children Placed in Office of Refugee Resettlement Care." https://oig.hhs.gov/oei/reports/oei-BL-18-00511.pdf

Donald J. Trump, Executive Order, "Affording Congress an Opportunity to Address Family Separation," June 20, 2018. https://www.whitehouse.gov/presidential-actions/affording-congress-opportunity-address-family-separation/

Human Rights Watch, "Turning Migrants into Criminals: The Harmful Impact of US Border Prosecutions," May 22, 2013. https://www.hrw.org/report/2013/05/22/turning-migrants-criminals/harmful-impact-us-border-prosecutions

Chapter Nine

Linda Qiu, "Border Crossings Have Been Declining for Years, Despite Claims of a 'Crisis of Illegal Immigration,'" *New York Times,* June 20, 2018. https://www.nytimes.com/2018/06/20/us/politics/fact-check-trump-border-crossings-declining-.html

Muzaffar Chishti and Michelle Mittelstadt, "Unauthorized Immigrants with Criminal Convictions: Who Might Be a Priority for Removal?," Migration Policy Institute, November 2016. https://www.migrationpolicy.org/news/unauthorized-immigrants-criminal-convictions-who-might-be-priority-removal

Chapter Ten

Chinese Exclusion Act. https://guides.loc.gov/chinese-exclusion-act

"Rock Springs Massacre: Topics in Chronicling America," Library of Congress. https://guides.loc.gov/chronicling-america-rock-springs-massacre

Massacre At Hells Canyon. https://www.opb.org/television/programs/oregon-experience/article/massacre-at-hells-canyon/

The Arid West - The Newlands Reclamation Act of 1902, Theodore Roosevelt Center at Dickinson State University. https://www.theodorerooseveltcenter.org/Blog/Item/The%20Arid%20West%20The%20Newlands%20Reclamation%20Act%20of%201902

The Blease Bill. https://immigrationhistory.org/item/
undesirable-aliens-act-of-1929-bleases-law/

Chapter Eleven

Sarah N. Lynch, Kristina Cooke, "Exclusive: U.S. Sending 1,600
Immigration Detainees to Federal Prisons," *Reuters*, June 7, 2018.
https://www.reuters.com/article/us-usa-immigration-prisons-
exclusive/exclusive-u-s-sending-1600-immigration-detainees-to-
federal-prisons-idUSKCN1J32W1

Global Detention Project Annual Report 2019, January
1, 2020. https://www.globaldetentionproject.org/
global-detention-project-annual-report-2019

"The Prison Industrial Complex: Mapping Private Sector
Players," Urban Justice Center's Corrections Accountability
Project, April 2018. https://www.prisonlegalnews.org/
media/publications/ThePrisonIndustrialComplex-
MappingPrivateSectorPlayersApril20185.pdf

Urban Justice Center's Corrections Accountability Project. https://cap.
urbanjustice.org

Monsy Alvarado, Ashley Balcerzak, Stacey Barchenger, Jon Campbell,
Rafael Carranza, Maria Clark, Alan Gomez, Daniel Gonzalez,
Trevor Hughes, Rick Jervis, Dan Keemahill, Rebecca Plevin, Jeremy
Schwartz, Sarah Taddeo, Lauren Villagran, Dennis Wagner, Elizabeth
Weise, Alissa Zhu, "These People are Profitable: Under Trump,
Private Prisons are Cashing in on ICEDdetainees," *USA Today*,
December 20, 2019. https://www.usatoday.com/in-depth/news/
nation/2019/12/19/ice-detention-private-prisons-expands-under-
trump-administration/4393366002/

Chapter Twelve

"COVID-19 Escalating in ICE Detention Centers as States Hit Highest Daily Records - and ICE Deportation Flights into Northern Triangle Continue," International Rescue Committee, August 3, 2020. https://www.rescue.org/press-release/covid-19-escalating-ice-detention-centers-states-hit-highest-daily-records-and-ice

Katya Schwenk, "The ICE Facility Where Almost Every Detainee Has Coronavirus," The American Prospect, August 12, 2020. https://prospect.org/justice/farmville-ice-facility-almost-every-detainee-has-coronavirus/

Aaron Reichlin-Melnick, "What You Need to Know About President Trump's Latest Ban on Immigration," Immigration Impact, April 23, 2020. https://immigrationimpact.com/2020/04/23/ban-on-immigration/#.X6LCiS2ZMWq

Muzaffar Chishti and Jessica Bolter, "Vulnerable to COVID-19 and in Frontline Jobs, Immigrants Are Mostly Shut Out of U.S. Relief," Migration Policy Institute, April 24, 2020. https://www.migrationpolicy.org/article/covid19-immigrants-shut-out-federal-relief

S.3548 CARES Act. https://www.congress.gov/bill/116th-congress/senate-bill/3548/text?q=product+actualización

Pandemic Unemployment Assistance. https://www.dol.gov/coronavirus/unemployment-insurance

Chapter Thirteen

Jens Manuel Krogstad, Jeffrey S. Passel and D'vera Cohn, "5 facts About Illegal Immigration in the U.S.," Pew Research

Center, June 12, 2019. https://www.pewresearch.org/
fact-tank/2019/06/12/5-facts-about-illegal-immigration-in-the-u-s/

Fourth Amendment, U.S. Constitution. https://constitutioncenter.org/
interactive-constitution/amendment/amendment-iv

Zadvydas v. Davis, 533 U.S. 678 (2001). https://www.loc.gov/item/
usrep533678/

Fifth Amendment, U.S. Constitution. https://constitutioncenter.org/
interactive-constitution/amendment/amendment-v

Chapter Fourteen

H.R. 1 Tax Cuts and Jobs Act, December 2017. https://www.congress.gov/
bill/115th-congress/house-bill/1

First Step Act (FSA) of 2018 (P.L. 115- 391), December 2018. https://www.
congress.gov/bill/115th-congress/house-bill/5682/text

Dominick Mastrangelo, "Lawyers Say They Can't Find Parents of 545
Migrant Children: Report," *The Hill*, October 10, 2020. https://thehill.
com/homenews/521978-lawyers-say-they-cant-find-parents-of-545-
migrant-children-report

Global Wealth Databook 2019, Credit Suisse. https://www.credit-suisse.
com/about-us/en/reports-research/global-wealth-report.html

Jonathan Ponciano, "The Countries with the Most Billionaires," *Forbes,*
2020. https://www.forbes.com/sites/jonathanponciano/2020/04/08/
the-countries-with-the-most-billionaires-in-2020/?sh=70b76f7e4429

"New Data Shows Immigrant-Owned Businesses Employed
8 Million Americans; Immigrants Wield $1.1 Trillion in
Spending Power," New American Economy, March 12,
2019. https://www.newamericaneconomy.org/press-release/

new-data-shows-immigrant-owned-businesses-employed-8-million-americans-immigrants-wield-1-1-trillion-in-spending-power/

2018 Hate Crime Statistics. https://ucr.fbi.gov/hate-crime/2018/hate-crime

"The Year in Hate and Extremism 2019," Southern Poverty Law Center, March 18, 2020. https://www.splcenter.org/news/2020/03/18/year-hate-and-extremism-2019

Aris Folley, "Hate Crimes Rose by 226 Percent in Counties Where Trump Hosted Campaign Rallies in 2016: Study," *The Hill*, March 23, 2019. https://thehill.com/blogs/blog-briefing-room/news/435458-hate-crimes-rose-by-226-percent-in-counties-where-trump

Chapter Fifteen

"Immigrant Founders of the 2017 Fortune 500," Center for American Entrepreneurship, December 2017. https://startupsusa.org/fortune500/

"Open for Business: How Immigrants Are Driving Small Business Creation In The United States," New American Economy, August 14, 2012. https://research.newamericaneconomy.org/report/open-for-business-how-immigrants-are-driving-small-business-creation-in-the-united-states-2/

Cesar Maximiliano Estrada, "How Immigrants Positively Affect the Business Community and the U.S. Economy," Center for American Progress, June 22, 2016. https://www.americanprogress.org/issues/immigration/news/2016/06/22/140124/how-immigrants-positively-affect-the-business-community-and-the-u-s-economy/

Muzaffar Chishti and Jessica Bolter, "Vulnerable to COVID-19 and in Frontline Jobs, Immigrants Are Mostly Shut Out of U.S. Relief," Migration Policy Institute, April

24, 2020. https://www.migrationpolicy.org/article/
covid19-immigrants-shut-out-federal-relief

Anca Spanu, "29 Percent of U.S. Doctors are Born Outside the U.S.,
New Study Shows," *Healthcare Weekly,* December 20, 2018. https://
healthcareweekly.com/u-s-doctors-new-study/

Rachel Iacono, Cristobal Ramón, "Immigrants in the Health
Care Workforce: An Explainer," Bipartisan Policy
Center, April 9, 2020. https://bipartisanpolicy.org/blog/
immigrants-in-the-health-care-workforce-an-explainer/

Julia Gelatt, "Immigrant Workers: Vital to the U.S. COVID-19
Response, Disproportionately Vulnerable," Migration Policy
Institute, March 2020. https://www.migrationpolicy.org/research/
immigrant-workers-us-covid-19-response

Chapter Sixteen

"Undocumented Immigrants' State & Local Tax Contributions," Institute
of Taxation and Economic Policy, March 1, 2017. https://itep.org/
undocumented-immigrants-state-local-tax-contributions-2017/